Thank

A Love
Suprem*e*

A Love Supreme

Brandon M. Graham

BROWNSTONE

For information regarding special discounts for bulk purchases, please contact Brownstone Publishing, Inc. at info@brownstonepublishing.com.

ISBN: 0-9728311-2-6 hardcover
ISBN: 0-9728311-3-4 paperback

2nd Edition March 2005

Printed in the United States of America
1. Poetry, 2. African-American, 3. Love, 4. Literature

Design and Layout: www.BudgetBookDesign.com
Editor: Cynthia Bingaman

Dedicated to Four Women,

To her who hath draped me in scarves of care
in times when my heart had grown wintry cold
To her who is the essential in my world
for she has breathed life into that which was living
Thus giving me new life
To her who has nursed my boyish dreams and aspirations
into manhood realities with love and truth
To her who has cultivated my very being with her presence
nurtured me and allowed me to grow
in the warmth of her sun and the sweetness of her rain

Acknowledgements

I wish to thank and acknowledge the following people and institutions who have made immeasurable contributions, whether it be time or financial support, to this project: The Creator; Ellis Graham for seeds planted; Liz Graham for cultivating hands; Patrick S. Graham for providing me with a better past enabling a brighter future (loving you with all I got; grand success is right around the corner); William A. Ampofo (CA$H) for continually raising the bar and achieving and re-raising and achieving and...; Alyssa; Nadia for patience; Ary (need I use words), Morgan & Graham Extended Family; Crosby High School; Upward Bound Program; National Association of Black Journalists; Liberty Mutual Insurance Group; The New York Times; The New Haven Register; The Waterbury Republican-American; The Spectrum Newspaper; RJ Communications; The Connecticut Post; The Hartford Courant; Dr. Curtis and the Sacred Heart University English Department; Don Cook and Sacred Heart University Athletic Department; Dr. Anthony Cernera and the extended Sacred Heart University community; Timothy C. Branner, II and the INROADS, Inc. Family; Pastor Vinny Lucian; Pastor Keith Stuarte and the Living Faith Christian Church Family; Pastor Bennett and the Mount Aery Baptist Church Family; The Wellington Family and Matah Network, Inc.; Keith Clinkscale and Vanguarde Media, Inc.; Dave Ogilvie and Higher Thought Publishing; Robert Trenske and RJT Pictures; Coach Arciero and CHS Football Family; Ironman Associates, LLC; BY FAM, Inc.; Hofstra Women's Basketball Crew; UCONN GIRLS – Turq, Jeronica, Dawn, Kelly; YALE CREW – Cherrilyn, Eryan, Kobe (homer-"doy"), Terrance; Xando's Café; Nuyorican Poets Café; Bar Nun; SCSU Poetry Crew and Blackout Crew; Mike McLaughlin and Lew DeLuca for taking a chance and changing my life; Coach Fleming for direction; Jasmin A. for a first kiss; Beatrice Perez for planting love; Tiana Carrasquillo for accepting the who I am; Sacred Heart University Football Family for support; Sacred Heart University Football Coaching Staff for discipline; Danielle for accompanying trains rides; Katie and Omar (the equation continues) for blankets, pillows, couches, second-floor floors, pop-tarts, showing me jersey, and teaching me that true love is color blind; William Pitt Foundation for enabling; Jim Barquinero for being an example of hard work; Deanna Fiorentino for understanding visions of high-rise buildings overlooking golf courses and city skylines and for understanding that *love actually* is all around (six-figure salary...I promise); Benjamin Robinson for making success tangible; Julie Savino for opportunity; Terry Walden for pearls of wisdom; Amina DeBurst for the convo and vegetarian paradise—what what!!! Ms. Divirgilio for planting the seed of literature; Kiheme Cowan; Jayson "Jay-Jerk" Jarrett (Spanish Town—me too!); Jamel Keels; Mr. Fred; Sr. Donna Dodge and Eileen Bertch; The Gibbs' Family; Kerryann Bryan for unforgettable Central Park visits and for hot summer days spent in Brooklyn apartments; William Mayeran for keeping s#@t straight; Basil Mitchell (you my na...rude boy!); Michele Walker (Chele) for D & D runs; Rume Pela for therapy?!?!; Amarlyn Diaz; Shellyann Johnson for D.C. trips; Dr. McAllister; Vikki Pryor for being an example and Dan Parker for perspective...best of luck homey; Keysha Whitaker; Mydria Clark; Faedra Bernier (many kisses and warm, mushy words); Ana Godoy for growth and development (all kinds, all kinds); Kia H20...shhh; Patrice Raffington for withstanding and holding true...I appreciate you more than...; Marissa L.—I love you and miss you terribly; Sean "Shaka" and the Mosque; Mrs. Purdy for teaching me the world is indeed a stage—I owe *this* to you with the deepest sincerity; Mr. Benevento; Ms. Kohwanoh, Dr. Gary Rose; Dr. Sid Gottlieb for imparting the importance of dialogue and film; Dr. DiPace for stressing the importance of relationships; Professor Nagy for encouragement, Professor Sweeney for poetry...ah...sweet poetry; Professor Mary Scroggins; Cam Farrar; Dave Carlor for intellectual workouts til 7:34am (young, black, and doing it); Sabine Auguste; Jill Fuller (I still have the letters); Chel'; and Greg Johnson. Big shout to cousin Dude (honorary graduate of Chesire Academy, Adelphi University, and George Washington University).

A special thanks to:

Marvin Royal for understanding normalcy and refusing to become it. You are my other intellectual half. I wish you the very best on your travels toward success. I'll see you at the top.

Marjorie Petit for everything and more...words cannot begin to describe your beauty, your friendship, your understanding, and your character. The love that I have for you transcends language so despite how many degrees I accumulate I'll never quite be able to articulate just how much I love you. Forever your friend, homey, and so much more. Best of luck on your journey, from the bottom of my soul's soul.

Saul Williams for the comfort I find in your voice and the camaraderie I find in your literature. Thank you for being a beautiful human being.

Nikki Giovanni for being my source of inspiration and my muse... Each day I thank the creator for your very existence and she smiles back at me with great delight.

exhaust the possibilities...

These are excerpts from Brandon M. Graham's essay *"Redefining A Love Supreme in the 21ˢᵗ Century"*. This will serve the purpose of giving the reader a clearer understanding and provide a key context.

Contents

FOREWORD

The primary aim of this collection is to lay a basic preliminary blueprint of my intellectual and poetic work. This volume assumes the structure of a variety of voices and serves as a concoction of an array of interests that focuses on three paramount themes: the art of loving, the difficulty of relational and social heartbreak, and the complexities encountered in the restoration of broken relationships.

My laborious pursuit for thoughtful understanding is a perpetually heartrending expedition. This attempt to excavate the core of the human existence, chiefly love, has caused me to encounter countless warm, richly intelligent souls who have been staggeringly open and generous in the giving of their time and the sharing of their thoughts. My social project of deepening the importance of relationships in a world drowning in capitalism, market-driven values, and the unwillingness to disabuse itself from the injuries incurred from class inequality, brutal state repression, widespread homophobia, rampant sexism, and racism is indeed an interminable process. This literary exploration serves to underscore the plight of both male and female inter-intimacy and accentuates the ever-evolving problems of racial inclusion and social injustice while broadening the scope of human dignity.

This body of work not only serves to epitomize the developmental progression of my thoughts on relational interaction, social degradation, and economic exploitation, but also preserves the authenticity of my own internal reflections on such issues. The selected poems were carefully chosen from my corpus of work to best represent the progression of my own societal observations and political criticisms tailored with viable solutions. And in my observation of societal issues, I find it impossible to divorce myself from my own criticisms and observations on what it means to be human, modern, American, black, male, and journeying toward better race relations, truth, and love.

I certainly hope the volume keeps these ideas alive in the mind of the reader, so that they may be debated, cultured, and polished in the academy and in the refineries of public dialogue across the globe. In my travels as a lecturer on the importance of literature and literacy as well as a performer of my own work, I am repeatedly confronted with the persistence of emotional exigent themes and concerns shared by my audiences. These include race, sex, relationships, but rather share a focus on the questioning of how one might attain true love, how one might avoid the emotional and psychological trappings of societal complacency that can lead to nihilistic behavior and despair, and lastly, how one might live more authentically. These intellectual encounters lead to constructive dialogue, exchanges of personal histories, and the obtainment of valuable knowledge. For these moments, I am eternally appreciative.

This collection of poetry I hope should serve as a literary rebuke to the ideology of life being an event of purely joy and happiness absent of toiling with the hardships of psychological stress, emotional sadness, and personal shortcomings. Despite the challenge of confronting life authentically, I wish for this collection to provide a context of how to enjoy the intimacies of a relationship while also preparing the reader for interludes of private and public heartbreak couched with amputated feelings. In addition, I hope to inspire those brave souls who wish to travel with me on this quest toward the romantic.

My work is a delicate struggle to be au fait with and respond to the discordant moan that is uttered from the souls of so many who are bemused and disoriented walking around in the quagmire of societal discontent. Failed love experiences, unrequited hope of government protection, and disillusions of societal acceptance into the mainstream have caused many to travel the road of nihilistic practice while contemplating physical, psychological, and spiritual suicide.

The existential quest I have embarked on toward finding meaning in life, love, and overall existence is just a feeble attempt to make sense of the world. However, it undoubtedly has also become a political and social struggle seated at the center of my thought. My writing moves violently toward finding healthy solutions on how to grapple with the challenges of living authentically, the attainment and preservation of love and relationships, battling with societal and self-sustained oppression and resistance, and the experience of genuine joy.

I am a Contemporary Intellectual Romantic with a profound allegiance to the exploration of the importance of relationships, sexual experiences, and the tear-soaked terrain of individual and societal heartache. By this, I mean I am fanatical about confronting the evils of baseless emotional sufferings that occur in relationships and the unnecessary social misery of a people, namely the black and brown underclass in America, but not limited to these two groups alone. This exploration is fueled by the need to grasp the reasoning behind what makes us so daring and courageous enough to fall in love and what makes us so spirited to war against social injustices at times while being so socially irresponsible and negligent at others. There are five fundamental questions that motivate my writings: What does it mean to be *in love*? Why are relationships so *important*? What does it mean to be *modern*? What does it mean to be *African American*? What does it mean to be *American*?

My grappling with such questions are deeply rooted in my own experience with love and observations of love and relationships. Another motivation that continues to bombard my thought is the constant brawling African Americans encounter with society daily. Identifying that we are all an anxiety-ridden, yet love-hungry people is also central in the development of themes in my work. I commend those who, despite pain and misery, immerse themselves in the salvation of embracing life's hopeful doctrines, individual and collective dreams, as well as valuable philosophic creeds. This makes life seem a bit more worth embracing.

To be American and in a relationship in the 21ˢᵗ century is to be part of a dialogical and semi-independence episode. There is an unremitting crusading of modernistic ideologies against conventional ones. Although being in a relationship is a romantic happening, in many cases, it is fanned and fueled by emotional emptiness, psychological dependence on others, which can stagger the growth of self, and furthermore by feelings of incompleteness. These qualities somewhat undermine relationships, especially romantic ones, and make them more of a fragile experiment.

This leaves a great many individual and societal questions unanswered in the dawn of the 21ˢᵗ century. Is true love possible in a capitalist, market-driven society? Is marriage a necessary experience in one's life? Are sexual emancipations what we need in America? Is religion a viable solution to attaining physical, psychological, and spiritual health? Do class, race, and gender hierarchy have the last word on how far democracy can go in our time?

"A love supreme" and our inability to recapture and sustain its existence in our own lives

In the first part of the book *A Love Supreme* I am attempting to explore and redefine love in the 21st century, while optimistically highlighting several of the expectations and prominent influences that are weighing in on us as we are challenged to interpret love, cast the players, and act out the storyline in our own lives.

The theme of physical and emotional satisfaction looms heavily in the allure of romantic love; it is even elevated in its beauty, centrally without fault because of the focus on sexual pleasure or verbal intimacy. These are two occurrences that happen when one is satisfied and/or understood; hence, the sense of loneliness becomes extinct. However, one must understand romantic love's elevation in the mind of a generation that strongly advocates sexual emancipations and same-sex marriages; we then begin to comprehend that this moral stance is highly subjected to the public criticism of our parents and/or conservatives, and conventional thought, not to mention being held under the pious microscope of stern religious criticism.

Religious heads will often offer negative criticism of sexual fulfillment outside the sanctity of marriage and speak to how many of the domestic instabilities and social ineptitudes directly result from our society basking in self-absorption during the heyday of modernity. Therefore, we have two polarized positions on how one should live his or her life: either be self-absorbed or be too dependent on societal acceptance. There does not seem to be, at least in present day America, a meeting ground of the two. These philosophies are completely polarized, without any force in sight that will bring them closer together in the hope of finding one that is healthy and existentially authentic.

Many people choose to embark on the tragic journey of romantic love for intellectual, existential, political, and psychological reasons. Nikki

Giovanni has taught us and liberation romantics remind us, a relationship in terms of an American one is especially fitted for the weak, lonely, and for many, psychologically troubled. Individuals tend to gawk at love subjectively or from below in this country. True romantic love or the ascension to the realm of what I define as "a love supreme" almost becomes caricaturized or likened to the ever-elusive carrot in front of the donkey. The donkeys, namely hopeless romantics, are persistent in that it they are perpetually in constant motion; however, there are no real gains being made in terms of the attainment of the carrot. It is rather inconsequential unless the inexorable persistence for one to be in motion or traveling toward something is looked upon as a favorable action.

Theoretically "a love supreme" is a fleeting state of existence by which one will experience the joy felt in the attainment of the emotional pinnacle of a relationship. However short-lived the experience, the visceral effects are long-term. Individuals will constantly journey in and out of relationships with the lone hope of regaining that divine sensation. "A love supreme" is pure and innocent. Many great thinkers of our day refer to it as brown sugar before it is granulated, processed, or refined. It invokes a universal love and quantifies a spiritual and emotional consciousness of the heart. Quite simply put: it is a magnificent moment, a monument of love in its purest, sweetest, and natural form.

Love implies intense fondness or deep devotion and may apply to various relationships. Affection suggests warm, tender feelings, usually not as powerful or deep as those implied by love. For men, in many instances, it is an epiphanic moment when he realizes his need for a woman in his life. There is an innate draw to her with the hope that she will save him from himself. This is an act of complete emotional submission.

In order for persons to attain "a love supreme," individuals need to strip themselves of the self-absorptive attitude, whose historical roots stem back to Ralph Waldo Emerson's famous lecture of 1837, "The American Scholar." Likened to this type of mother country dominance over island methodology, individuals need to liberate themselves from their slavish dependence on societal acceptance. This ideal principally emanates from millenniums of male-dominated societies where women were affixed to the role of the subservient partner of the male. After centuries of societal grooming, this has lead to the psychological/emotional dependence women have on a male to service the roles of a partner and protector. One must understand that, in terms of a relational market-place, only in recent history have women begun to sexually and relationally emancipate themselves and crop a different produce of independence. Hopefully, with the growth of female independence, men and women can work well together toward achieving a healthy reliance on each other in society.

However, with modern-day American culture's preoccupation with break-ing us away from each other, one cannot assume that this public under-taking will be an easy one. As disheartening as it may be, the situation needs to be addressed. The individual search for relational identity can only begin to find purpose or resonate with people who naturally sense, experience, and feel interconnected with other humans organically, because they recognize that for them, it is a pure progression of exis-tence to feel kin, and to value the importance of relationships. The expe-rience of natural acceptance and the sense of belongingness is a happening, if you will, that cannot be duplicated by grandiose cere-monies of matrimony, or internally with the distribution of drugs or medication to numb the pain or fill the void. One does not need cere-monies such as marriage to solidify the bold declaration of acceptance.

Amputated feelings as they relate to sexual and relational problems, class injustice, and social heartbreak

In the second section of the text, *Amputated Feelings*, I am attempting to unearth the complexities of relational and social heartbreak. Social heartbreak occurs when individuals feel an immense amount of anger, sadness, and/or frustration, and essentially have no means by which to channel these consuming, destructive emotions. Within a social context, these feelings centrally come about given that individuals feel their education, hard work, and determination are unrequited by society's promise of success and acceptance in America.

Success and acceptance is so problematic because it is usually defined by individual's standards, but interrupted by mass media, failing educational systems, and governmental approval. The acknowledgement of social heartbreak is an epiphanic realization for individuals when they comprehend that they may be, in fact, marginalized and excluded from opportunities and from important conversations ongoing in America, as if to say, "you are not important enough and your voice does not count." This, in turn, creates a conscious binaural fixture. The consciousness is dealing with both the hatred felt for the elitist and as well as a raging hatred against self. There is an overwhelming sense of hopelessness, namelessness, and invisibility that is confirmed by elitist groups and government distancing themselves from a people. This invents an impression of social abandonment, which propels this intergenerational cycle of hate and walking nihilistic behavior, further producing physical, sexual, and emotional violence, causing a breakdown in community and largely, American society. Hence, we have individuals, and collectively a people, who are socially heartbroken.

Social heartbreak can cause individuals and/or people to entertain sporadic behavior such as random acts of violence and suicide attempts. One flagship example of this is the 1992 LA Riots. Here, we have a group people rioting and committing random acts of criminal activity and violence toward whites within their community. What is most shocking about this occurrence is that the rioting takes place in one's own neighborhood. This is a comprehendible example of self-destructive behavior, which serves as a centerpiece in the diagnosis of a people more or less running in the streets of Los Angeles, consumed by nihilism.

When intelligently examining this type of behavior of a people, one must grasp and fully understand that nihilistic behavior does not come about from a nonentity, but that it is rather a reaction or a consequence of a malevolent social condition. And what makes this country so interesting is how we have always fumbled away practical solutions when approaching social repression and social heartbreak that results in social disconnect, even though we have been dealing with these sicknesses from our country's inception. American society has always been chronically racist, sexist, homophobic, and nationalistic when convenient (post-9/11 era). A distinctive characteristic of this country is that race has always served as a staple in the nation's pursuit of its own identity.

Even within the past 50-60 years, there has been a response of movements for racial, class, and sexual equality. Although insufficient, it has certainly brought issues into the ongoing political and societal discourse. The reasoning behind why these movements have been insufficient perhaps may be because they act as band-aids, when in actuality, America is in deep need of social and political surgery. However, we as a country probably do not have the sufficient moral coverage needed in our ethical insurance policies to handle the cost of moral, societal, and political reconstructive surgery. Band-aids may heal the wound cosmetically, but what lies untouched, not properly assessed and treated, or even in the political sense, un-interrogated, have been the maldistribution of wealth, land, and power in American society. Yet the government and elitist groups do not want to have an open and honest *tête-à-tête* on such topics for fear that they would, in fact, lose the leverage and control that they presently exercise over a virtually powerless people.

The amputation of feelings and the discomforting sensation of social disconnect stems from an underclass', namely blacks and browns, inability to love themselves. Again, these feelings are a direct consequence of the malevolent social conditioning of four hundred and fifty-four years of slavery, despite the so-called abolition of slavery with Lincoln's Emancipation Proclamation. After the Emancipation Proclamation, blacks still endured institutionalized domestic terrorism in the form of lynching, segregation, and countless other methods coursed toward cheapening the value of their existence. These white, dehumanizing activities have left their toll on blacks, causing emotional and psychological scarring, and personal wounds now inscribed on the *souls of black folk*. Walking nihilism is a direct result of such circumstances. These conditions make any qualitative human relationship hard to maintain, especially personal relationships between races.

The dismantling of the black family is largely due to the fact of the disproportionate number of black males being sent to prison. The removal of the male head of the black family leads to a social breakdown of the black family and on a greater scale, American society. This leaves a class of African Americans, mainly lower to middle class ones, who are insecure, willing to be co-opted by and incorporated into the powers that be, concerned with racism to the degree that it poses constraints on upward social mobility. This longing to feel accepted into mainstream American society contributes to the desertion of the aforementioned black underclass that embodies a kind of walking nihilism of pervasive drug addiction, pervasive alcoholism, pervasive homicide, and an exponential rise in suicide.

These temptations that are bilking away the freedoms of so many blacks are chiefly due to the structural and institutional forces that are at work: namely unemployment, the failed educational system, and the consumer culture that bombards them (black consumer spending is estimated around 600 billion dollars a year +/-5%). The black underclass still has to contend with all of these bombardments in addition to a larger racist legacy. When a group of people is confronted with such a daunting reality, it can only be reflected in moral outrage. The African American inclusion into mainstream American society has been and still proves to be difficult. With all these external pressures, how can individuals love themselves, their family, and/or a significant other? And without healthy relationships, there will be a breakdown in self, family structure, and community. This is a problem worth dealing with as Americans.

Prosthetic apologies as they relates to Relational & Societal Resurrection

On the commencement of this already disquieting century, a peculiar impression of terror and optimism preoccupies us. We can certainly remember the malicious attacks on our country on September 11, 2001 and the irksome circumstances that have risen since with the war on terrorism and more pointedly, the war in Iraq. Nevertheless, let us not forget the heroic energies of those who have braved the battlefront under the presumption of defending homeland security and the democratic values we seek to uphold.

My work and the way I live my life has always sought to pay homage to the romantic who finds oneself desperately, despairingly in search of love and engagement in thoughtful socio-philosophic dialogue while voyaging toward the idea of democracy. The work has been my personal passion, an unswerving march toward the idea of keeping alive an unassuming nature about being an intellectual, and with bated breath the embodiment of the idea of a shared hope of societal betterment.

As unwelcoming as the outlook appears to be, there are a few viable solutions to attempt to reconcile broken relationships. In terms of racial inclusion, I believe that love can be the thread that interweaves various races, ethnicity, and cultures into the American fabric. This will inherently lead to better race relations. At the root of this concept is the belief that individuals must be willing to listen and dialogue with each other. Dialogue careers a true openness about emotions, feelings, and misconceptions that have been repressed either out of ignorance or fear. Love liberates the handicap placed on the discussion of race in America. Until we have this discussion on a national level, initiated by education, institutionalized by government, and practiced by citizens, race relations will not improve. Racial antagonism unravels American unification, advocating racial discrimination and segregation (this practice is also true of male-female relationships), two corpses we have been attempting to bury for generations and have met with little success in light of the

Civil Rights Movement, which was somewhat liberating not only for blacks and browns in this country, but for women, too.

The formulaic concept of prosthetic apologies stems from the medical profession's procedure by which prosthetic devices are utilized and put in place to aid or replace an absent body part with the hope of regaining function. These devices are designed, manufactured, and adjusted to fit a particular individual.

The basis of this idea holds true for emotions as well. In relationships, there are many incidents that result in feeling hurt, causing sadness and heartbreak. What occurs when individuals experience severe insensitivity is that feelings are figuratively amputated. This is to say that feelings are not merely hurt, but more accurately, there is an acute emotional disconnect between both parties in the relationship. They are emotionally disengaged.

The party responsible may be weighed with feelings of emotional guilt, resulting in an attempt to salvage the relationship; they will make an effort to restore the bond to its original state, usually without success, by offering an apology. Nonetheless, this is how we arrive at the concept of prosthetic apologies, a simple act of trying to re-establish the emotional state through acts of contrition. The challenge that is presented here is that prosthetics, in the physical or emotional realm, are never one-hundred-percent successful in restoring stability to a body or to a relationship.

At which point we then should be obliged to grasp a deeper understanding of what it means to be in love after encountering heartbreak. To be in love in the 21st century is to be interlaced into this ever-evolving conversation that is going on in America about how individuals are relentlessly grappling with the challenge of being in relationships in a liberal society. This almost becomes a project of social experimentation. Although America does romanticize love, the media outlets here fan and fuel the projected image in a more fundamental sense, which results in the aforementioned experiment becoming all the more fragile and polluted. Despite the brittleness of the experiment, individuals enlist to participate because America lends influence and enormity to the possibility that future relationships can, in fact, trump past or present mishaps.

Being a romantic with strong non-marital commitments, I am fixated with encountering the insidious evils of human life and the unrequited expectations of romantic love. There is a fascination, in a non-masochistic manner, with braving the romantic terrain of relationships and exploring life outside of the marital union because one wishes to attempt to live authentically. This is not to say that one cannot live authentically while being married, but rather to offer social commentary on the actuality that many, in fact, in this day in age, do marry out of peer and family expectancy, societal pressures in regards to status, and out of a sense of hopelessness. Many believe that misery does love company. My retort to these flawed decisions is to encourage people to wait and be patient in life and have faith, in a non-religious sense, that the union of one and his/her partner is a natural progression of life.

I am very intrigued with the whole notion of people falling in love with people they have known for a long time. The whole idea of seeing someone you have known for years suddenly, not instantaneously— more so progressively, being seen in a different romantic light is romantically inspiring. Or there is this progressive realization of how one has felt all along about that individual. The notion is very intriguing and terribly romantic, I think. The evolution of relationships seems more practical. In America, we are so keen on the "now" and the fulfillment of the self straight away; we neglect the need for closer inspection.

In contrast, I believe to be a true romantic is to possess heroism and to employ one's judicious intelligence to probe, examine, and challenge, in non-literary terms, the prevailing contemporary authorities on romanticism, that do, in fact, pressure us to indulge in "here today, gone tomorrow" relationships that are romantically anticlimactic, leaving us intel-lectually dissatisfied, spiritual unrequited, and sexually fulfilled, but that feeling is extremely perishable. And to surrender to sophomoric feel-ings is a failure of strength, lack of closer intellectual inspection, and relatively, a succumbing to wholesale sexual propaganda; in my mind, a best-selling product of a capitalist, market-driven value system.

In contrast to what is to indulge in self pleasures of contemporary roman-tic ideas is the distinguishing indicators of a true romantic. One who is fearless to trail the trek of intimate, fecund dialogue despite the proba-ble confrontation with fallible inquiry and authentic intimacy before engaging in a romantic relationship is, again, very socially inspiring and should be commended. These fruitful verbal exchanges are absolutely critical when laying a sound foundation in any relationship. Without the attentive laying of the foundation in a relational sense, the superstruc-ture is handicapped, weakened, and in most cases, doomed to stultify the growth of the relationship.

I

a   love   supreme

Brandon M. Graham

tracing (kindergarten love)

the art of loving you
has always been so very complex
consequently, i've decided to reduce it
to the simplicity held in the likeness
of childish finger-painting, fat-crayon coloring,
and the steady hand involved in tracing

and from working with my own,
i've learned that
those two things you call your hands
in fact are not hands at all
but two delicate brown crayons
softly tracing across the surface of my skin

and if i were a teacher
and you were my student,
all that i would ask
is that you please continue to stay within
the boundaries of my body,
but incessantly practice loving me
outside the lines of commonality

on painting

she resembles the beauty of my past

a visually arresting portrayal
of what i used to paint
with fingertips and watercolors
in the dreams of my childhood
she is a mirrored image of physical finery
classically framed

she now personifies the philosophy
of what beauty grew to be
inadvertently, she incarnates the complexities
of simple beauty defined,
all the while causing me
to study and excavate the intricacies
of why i even deserve her
uncategorically, she has been classified as
the treasured embodiment of a distinctive innocence
molded by the hands of celestial creativity

to call her, name her, an angel
would be an understatement

words cannot contain her beauty,
nor define it

hence, i've taken a buddhist 10-year vow of silence...

and now only paint her with the written word

necessity (the sweetest oxygen)

as a patient   *[pause]*   patiently awaiting her arrival
i stood as a child
hands pressed, face pressed against the window of my pain
and though i had no issue of blood
just issues of the heart
i had hoped my faith would enable me to become whole again
she wore not garments of clergy,
nor was she encircled in the midst of a crowd
but i knew it was all in touch,
her single-handed clutch that could nurse my pain
thus, i would be made whole again

mother should have named her physician

in her touch alone she had intoxicated me
caused me to host visions in dizzying spells
of untold tales of how i'd always wanted to be loved
of how i'd always needed someone
to nurse this broken heart
to nurse these scars

*[silence. enters a beautiful girl wearing a head-wrap,
four-inch black heels, carrying a small, black and blue
designer bag stuffed with dreams deferred]*

i thought aloud:
she comes in the form of the sweetest oxygen
and has breathed life into that which was living
thus, giving me new life

she enables me to recognize that i had been dead
far longer than i had been living

my thoughts became paralyzed
and as i laid there in a trance
i attained a new standard of *under   stand   ing*
which had been unknown to me
i suddenly
comprehended theorems of what exactly love is
and i drew the most beautiful conclusions
on a pad of loose leaf thought
acknowledging that her love had defied all the verbiage
Webster could muster
definitions would not only
confine her
but would fail to
define her

bravery warred against insecurities

and although her heart
had felt and known all too well the shackles
of
heartache
of
heartbreak
she   *[pause]*   loved me wholly

despite all the matters of the heart
she had chosen to love me so freely
she had me wide open,
wild loose like a pair of old hand-me-down trousers
i then silently recognized to self that
she was the lone reason why gray skies had become foreign

why skies had resumed blue
her rays of care had shone so passionately down on me
and i'd felt for the first time in all of my existence
as if i, too, were a   *[pause]*

necessity

as she smiles...

she smiles as if...

the sun is never going to set
as only the buoyancy and the resilient optimism of a woman can

but night was soon to come

so i in an attempt
to preserve the happiness of her soul
i quickly gathered ancient sun dials, clocks,
and all the wasted moments of time;
battled Cronos 'til death
and i...
i even handcuffed seconds,
imprisoned minutes, and executed hours

and time was no more

and as of late
i've begun to recognize that her happiness
seems to be as consistent as the golden sky
suddenly reminding me
that there is no greater pleasure
than the sweetness that resides in her smile

as she smiles...back at me

an ode: to a woman of a darker shade

i've got this jones
    for a woman of a darker skin tone
she has awakened within me
    a passion buried underneath years of resentment
she has returned me so sweetly back to my innocence
    with folded hands and knees bent
so sincerely prizing her existence more so
    than a *day of rue* for those seeking penance
as blake, i too, wonder whose hands could but
    frame thy fearful symmetry
complexion tinted with a darker shade of beauty
    accompanied by those almond-shaped eyes
filled to the brim with such mystery
    her beauty is deservéd of the highest praise
likened to that ushered by the greeks in the earliest of morns
    and understand that our separation is like
nails piercing through my limbs
    i, then, releasing screams from the pressing thorns
your appearance continuously thwarting those questioning
    the beauty found within your tonality
totally oblivious, i'm feeling you in totality
    i mean, nubian goddess, you've got a hold on me
got my heartbeat beating speedily like hands to a djembe
    seriously, euro-art could not compare to thee
i embrace thy large nose and thou wide hips
    as well as those lips that are so full of seduction
i wish to live seventy lives of those in a seven-year sleeper's
    den with the solitary thought of you alone   *[pause]*
without interruption; forget not my love,

even in your darkest hour that i've
    offered thanks to the creator   *[pause]*
for you have been my steadfast lover and my blessed angel
    and i hope never to be freed, but to lie in great contentment
caught in thy web, wishing to be forever entangled

early mornings

i actually always look forward
to our early morning valedictions
cause it is only then
that i can lie alone in the sheets
where we made love
the night before
and inhale the sweet aroma
of the sweat that dripped
from your shoulder blade
and trickled from behind your knee
in those close moments of ecstasy
when it seemed as if there were two
but we, knowing all too well,
knew that we had become one
and i was so into you   *[pause]*

and that's not just an r&b phrase

joy (rume)

in search of it
i found you

the thought of you
causes my heart to smile
with the sincerity held in the happiness
of a
childhood memory

free will

if in fact there did exist
the theoretical concept of free will
i'd be sure to exercise mine daily
praying to a new god
asking for death today,
resurrection tomorrow
only to be then reincarnated
in your likeness
in your image

instead of god's

(she, she, and i all smirked)

completion (for my missing piece)

3:47 a.m.

it's usually in the wee hours

sometime in between the rising of the sun
and the beginning of my morning

that she comes to mind

usually e-mails are drafted
and redrafted but never sent
numbers are dialed but phone calls are rarely ever placed
feelings are felt but never actually conveyed
because of insecurities surrounding rejection

but it's her—it's her
that transcends boyish dreams and collegiate crushes
there's hints of sincerity that i'd rather not keep to self
although knowing that i should

but i'm a liberal
a democrat by default
and i've never really believed in censorship of any sort
so i put fingertips to keyboard keys

and think to myself "uhmm...i'll try again"

because i'm drawn to her like...like...
forgone conclusions
and we've already met

so there's no need for an introduction
and she's already the em *[bodi]* ment of my everything
so i've concluded that she's my missing conclusion

without her, i'm an essay of life...so incomplete

and when asked why
i stutteringly reply:
it...it's the darkness of her hair
the dimness held in her eyes
and the glow of her cheekbones
that peak through the window
of my patternized-mundaness
allowing me to live at all
visions of her face accompany me
wherever i travel along this tragic journey called life

she is the embodiment of the hope in my daymares
and the personification of
the frightening satisfaction that i seek in my nightdreams

she makes me question the validity of my own existence
so i attempt to ignore her
like a distant memory of a hurtful past
but she comes back
she always comes back like...air
she ever surrounds me
refreshes me   enables me

she sustains my existence

most thoughts come to shape around her lips
scented with the softness of her breath,
felt with the warmth of her character,

heard with the grace in her walk
and seen by the voice held in her intelligence

suddenly reminding me
that my day has not yet begun
until she smiles over at me
calling the sun into action,
the flowers to yawn awaking,
and the birds to sing

making me feel so completely unincomplete

she puzzles me and completes me
in so many ways
on so many levels

and for that i thank her

i like...us

i like long strolls through good literature on muggy summer afternoons i like to draw hot baths on cold wintry evenings when things get too complicated i like massaging your shoulders and caressing the gentleness of your inner forearm because you've carried us for so long i like rubbing your back whenever you feel the need and washing your feet with the softness of my hair i like drinking the sweetness from your breast and bathing in your nile, huddling in the safety of your congo, while embracing the heat of your desert because you are so much more than a black woman, a black mother, a black sister, a black aunt...your scent alone is a remnant of home

i'm remembering mother africa

i like our people for our faith in the unseen and our hope in the hopeless and our trust in the untrustworthy because for some strange reason we, as a people, have this crazy notion that humanity is kind and loving despite our troubled past with those of lighter shades and i very much like you, and you, and you probably would like to remember our growth being stifled by the master and not the slave

yes?

i like those who have rejected the idea that we are an uncivil, ignorant, and intellectually inferior people i applaud you for believing that there can be, should be, must be, and somehow find the resources to create change, if not for all, then definitely for some and i cannot explain just how difficult it is for us to laugh when trying not to cry; to continue praying to a christian god when remembering our troubled past or just how difficult it is to lend momentary-lifted grins in order to shield our most secure insecurities and i very much like you, like you must gain an understanding that our remembrance of slavery is not a pleasant one but an absolute necessity

but this poem is not an angry poem

and if thought to be, this poem itself apologizes for that because i like you, like the way our grandmas, mothers, aunts, sister-cousins rise before the sun and fold loads of last night's laundry without a single complaint while preparing breakfast for families still asleep in the comforting silence of a house not yet awake ever so still

or perhaps it's the way our grandfathers, fathers, uncles, brother-mans stagger home, returning from working third shifts just in time to see their wives off to work and children off to school only to begin the cycle over again the same night we become so disconnected

however, i certainly applaud those of us who have challenged or disregarded comments by those which are meant to make us feel insecure, inferior, and even question the validity of our own existence because we are a beautiful people and i like the way we've come to terms with ourselves and have joined together in the celebration of the who that we are and the glorious who we are sure to soon become, so i like the way we celebrate ourselves despite their attempt to disproportionately incarcerate our men, pimp our women, and brainwash our children

but this poem is not an angry poem

because i like very much the way we tend our own without the proper education, monies, resources, or opportunities but you may not wish to remember those parts of our american history cause it brings back so much pain and anguish, hate and disgust and i've got to be honest...even i at times don't want to *re member*

[pause]

cause even i, at times,
don't want to re   *member*
i don't want to re   *member*
living in poverty
i don't want to re   *member*
going hungry or being cold
i don't want to re   *member*
sounds of gunshots
i don't want to re   *member*
sneakers hanging from power lines
i don't want to re   *member*
the smell of alcohol
i don't want to re   *member*
doo-rags, timberland boots,
air jordans, starter jackets, and gold chains
i don't want to re   *member*
being told i was too dark
i don't want to re   *member*
words like "nigger"
i don't want to re   *member*
being   *[looooooong pause]*   black
i don't want to re   *member*
being

but then she smiles, she being black woman, and he cannot help but to
smile, so he, too, smiles, he being black man, and black man being i,
and i suddenly remember that *i like…us* for all the simple reasons and
that's more than enough and so we journey on together

and if i might add, i like even more the sight of brown children playing on
newly built playgrounds in undeveloped urban settings on midsummer
afternoons while sipping on quarter waters or chewing on penny candy

or maybe it's just the sight of

brown children knowing happiness
and not yet understanding poverty

or maybe it's just the sight of

brown children knowing happiness
and not yet understanding poverty

but whatever the reason is,
i know i kind of like it and for these reasons…i like us

*this has been a brief moment in black history paid for by your attention. thank you.

nourishment: flawless indian depiction

i kissed you
and bled happiness that flowed like rivers
of unsuspected shivers
i then cupped my emotions
and imbibed the sweetest nectar
that speedily spread throughout my being
like some form of uncontrollable liver cancer
consuming me whole; even dance a sun dance with my very soul

kissing you taught me how
to tongue-kiss the sun without becoming burnt
how to inject uv rays without becoming addicted
i then realized all these years i'd been
desperately in need of some form of   *heroine*
got that seven-year itch
desperately seeking that fix
longing to lick those lips
that drip spit sweeter
than caribbean sugar cane
coppertone queen, draped in indian commitment
caused happiness to spring up inside of me
coming as an unexpected rain
coming as a much needed rain

i shall never thirst again

i tasted you
and my belly had begun to swell
more full than the moon
i swallowed visions whole
of being entangled in your warm embrace
my thought hosted visions of your lovely face
i eyed you from afar and have sat for days in a drunken trance
foolish to think that i could engulf
but more than one glance
of your beauty
you have caused my thoughts to dance
dances only known to one's past
i've been dry for years but i couldn't resist
so i placed you on ice
and consumed yet another glass

i shall never thirst again

time (she is)

if she were time
i'd be content existing
as but a single moment
in the ever-expanding span of her essence
and i being of moment
in an attempt to secure my livelihood
i'd pull the plugs on every clock
in every city, every state, every country,
and on every continent
and stop the tick and tock of every watch
on every wrist

i'd blind the sun with uv rays
swallow the moon whole

there would be no day or night just a long stretch of time

i'd reverse the future
fast-forward the past
paused in the eternal stillness of the now, now
resting peacefully assured in this single solitary moment
just the way that it is

my joy has a funny tendency
to be as continuous as her smile

but there's this entity called time
which seems to be overly concerned
with the yesterdays of days to come
and the tomorrows of our past
but i can't seem to get beyond the now

and the way you massaged my shoulders with seconds
and planted minutes on my cheek
while rubbing hours across my lower spine
until eternity was finite and i was rested

her smile is soothing like suicide after the discovery of truth

girl
(for a cuban-shaded brown girl)

without seed, soil, water, or sunlight

you grew me

you grew me with kisses underneath streetlights
on the corner of 51st between park and madison

you grew me

you grew me while we were carefully sipping cups of coffee
in coffee lounges while lounging comfortably
in words volleyed during intimate conversations

you grew me

tactic

instead of playing eyetag

we played hide and go seek
she hid behind her emotional wall of insecurity

and i being persistent
and groomed in intellectualism
i frantically thumbed through history books
studied the reagan administration
sought out periodicals on east german history from november 9, 1989

and planned a tactic of my own
(ready or not here i come)

simple reasons

it's for all the simple reasons

it's the unfamiliarity of her kiss
that facilitates the preservation of sleepless nights
it's the untried trail of her skin i've yet to explore
that peeks through the window of my curiosity daily
it's the foreign happiness i genuinely feel when i see her
it's the nameless emotion that bubbles inside me when she smiles
it's the mystery of her scent that draws me closer

it's the comfort i feel from her glare as she stares
halfway hoping to be caught looking over at me
as i'm halfway hoping to be caught looking over at her

it's for these reasons alone that i am reminded
why i'm so intrigued...oh so intrigued...

it's for all the simple reasons

why? (she asked)

i love you without explanation,
or any kind of a simple derivation
i love you because your very existence
is the sole causation
for the formulated concept *[pause]*
of love

and if it's any kind of consolation
my love for you is not to be held
in question
suspicion,
or by the hands of anyone else for that matter

man

he wanted to be a brick
but she refused to be the mortar
and despite not laying a sound foundation
they continued to build

he wanted to be her light
but she chose to be the absence of
and his days grew darkly dim

he wanted to be her addiction
so he became a cigarette
not knowing she had given up smoking for lent

he thought to try her addictions once more
and became religion
but she'd gone off to school and became an atheist

he tried to be music
but she wouldn't listen

he wanted to be her business
but she said the overhead was too costly

he wanted to become
an army of two
but she refused to enlist *(i suppose we can blame bush)*

he simply wanted to be hers
but her credit score indicated
that she was in no position to own anything

so he decided to become
a man
and she, knowing they belonged,
she then became a woman

and they became one

she died a year later and he soon followed her,
believing in the afterlife

fruit

it must've been the softness of her palm
gently stroking the stubble of my beard
in concert with the shyness of her glare

or quite simply, it's the relief i feel
when she smiles
that suddenly reminds me
why adam really had no choice
but to partake of the fruit

she has a funny way of controlling
these uncontrollable feelings i have for her

she e (astrological love)

she had the most beautiful cinnamon complexion
mine eyes had ever seen
i was lusting to love her infinitely
without any "i need my own space"
remarks in between

her words were like strands of a comforter
wrapping around me
in the midst of our conversation,
to be more exact;
her words were like a healing balm
being placed on a mental abrasion
she was not less than, more than
but quite simply,
she was my equal in this equation

she had become so much more
than the one i desired to hold
she was my shepherd
and i faithfully became her fold

i began following her
as does the dreamer follow the wind
i've even asked god
if i could be recreated in her image instead of hers
if i ever decided to become born again
(and that's not just a theological statement)
she was the fresh embodiment
of everything i've ever wanted
she became my soul's twin

we ascended and starred the northern sky
and god named us gemini

we were astrologically in love

admiration

i certainly think you have to admire those who push shopping carriages into their proper place in those half-full grocery parking lots on those muggy summer afternoons all simply because customers believe that if they exercise their right to make someone else's job a bit less stressful, then they would be defying the fundamental principle of americanism, and that would not only be doing a disservice to themselves but to the american people as a whole, and come to think of it, i would agree that all people who practice americanism deserve some type of badge, medal, purple heart, or at least some formal honorary doctoral degree from an ivy league institution   *[pause]*   i mean, wouldn't you agree, mr. president?

and i certainly am a strong believer that there should be an echoing round of applause for mothers everywhere who slave in kitchens over hot stoves and lukewarm dishwater, all so that their families can be nourished and be well accustomed to cleanliness, and we all know that cleanliness is biblical. and if my mother, who just so happens to be a christian missionary, says that being a housewife or a homemaker is in fact a calling or ministry in and of itself, i thought i ought to do the good christian thing and at least acknowledge it in a poem or some type of strong opinionated editorial. but i suppose this will do. i hope she smiles when she reads this.

and i, therefore, call for a day of admiration for men everywhere, especially fathers. some may say that we have father's day to honor these men, but i think there should be a special holiday for fathers everywhere who fix vacuum cleaners on early tuesday evenings because the ol' faithful kirby decided that it didn't want to pick up, or maybe it was the children who decided not to, but nonetheless, if you look hard enough and long enough and perhaps even if you peer through windows in metropolitan projects or suburban condominiums, you'll find fathers stretched out on the ground, fixing vacuum cleaners, and i thought that if we couldn't get congress to pass a bill for a holiday, i at least would like to acknowledge these men with some type of thank card...(well, this is mine)

and i think it's certainly agreeable that we, as a people, should give standing ovations to those who work third shifts, who drive around in an '84 toyota because car notes would be too much of a burden seeing that a vehicle comes second, no third, no, actually fourth, to food, clothes, and shelter. and if you are a supporter of ms. hillary clinton (yes, i wrote ms. and it's not a typo), then education also, because she, too, believes as the african proverb goes, "it takes a village to raise a child," and about some nonsense of "no child being left behind," but i can't seem to understand why so many children of color are living in villages where people don't care and why so many children of color are sent off to schools that are overcrowded, drug infested, and unsafe, and where there are not enough textbooks. i mean, how would you like to read from a 224-page book that has been xeroxed and stapled chapter by chapter? and i certainly think there is something to be said about young black and brown boys and girls who matriculate into these predominantly white campuses in an attempt to and with the hope of creating change. i hope you're standing when reading this.

my flame

the reasons i love you so much
are your warm kisses and your gentle touch
i wish we could be together every second of the day
every night that's the prayer i pray
my heart has a desperate cry for your love
like a companion for a lonely dove
you are as beautiful as the bright blue sky
i'll cherish your love 'til the day that i die

i will love you in the future
i loved you in the past
i would give you the world
if that be the question you ask
my love runs deeper than the ocean blue
every white moon and black night i dream of you
i hope someday we will share the same last name
because your love is the fire which ignites my flame

brown girls

i like brown girls
   with nice, round, brown bottoms
      in brown, low-cut levi's jeans
         with halter tops
            that don't reveal
               too much of that divine brown bosom
               all the while
                  flaunting those cute, brown bellybuttons
                  just enough to make brown boys
                     in light-brown sweat pants   *[pause]*

pant

i like brown girls with thick brown thighs
   in thin, brown summer dresses
      with cute brown toes
         who take long strolls
            through brown sand on brown beaches
               with a brown brother in their left hand
               and a brown handbag in their right
                  or just the concept of a brown girl
                     having a brown brother in any hand
                     kinda seems, kinda feels

right   *[pause]*   anyhow

a conversation between men

o: okay, good point, but what if race didn't matter, then would you?

b: but...but it does.

o: for the sake of arguing, what if it didn't?

b: uhmm...okay, but that's almost like saying, if gender didn't matter, then you would fuck me? right?

awkward truths

awkward silence

reina: flawless latina depiction

light-skinned beauty
nameless coloured girl
walking dauntlessly through
the hallways of my vision
creation marked its finest decision
with tongues that roll r's like
the rolling tops of *el yunque*
i look upon you
as if in the stead of clay
god had chosen
to use vanilla, pinched
with the sweetest nutmeg,
thus began the molding
of the most sensual legs
each standing like pillars
of some ancient mayan temple
where many gather at thy feet
and usher in the highest praise
likened to that ushered in by ancient greeks
in the earliest of morns
sacrifice grew custom
to love you i'd offer my firstborn
as i continued to kneel
i hummed hymns of worship
in total awe of this girl
who possessed a face that could
set the sail of ten thousand warships
helen of troy could not compare to thee

ships in flight, all desperately seeking
to possess thy love
and i, too, wish to hold you
in my warm embrace
and taste from thy lips
the drip of spit sweeter
than caribbean sugar cane
i simply long to taste
and to never thirst again
i imbibed the sweetest nectar
that warmed me from within
cupped my hands
and drank the sweetest latino libation
foreign to all men

faulty craftsmanship
is unknown to thee
for god hath molded you
with divine care
flawless latino depiction
eye cannot help but to stare
those inked of a lesser melanin
look upon thee with an envious glare
that tell tales of little latino girls
learning to tuck their accents behind their backs
of another generation
and being sent to speech class
where they were handed glass after glass
until they all lay intoxicated
in self-made pools of vomit
that smelled and tasted
a whole lot like standard english
some had drowned
they being chastised by grandmothers

who never bothered to learn;
grandma used to grab bars of soap
attempting to wash
the *eng lish* off their tongues
which oftentimes
stung more than it burned
she wishing granddaughters
spoke *eng less*[2]

notes headed home read
and i quote
"my teacher can't understand what i spoke"
end quote
they not yet understanding that
The Words Don't Fit in My Mouth
but still
they persist on shoveling down our throats
those old english-coated viles of
A-E-I-O-U
A-E-I-O-U
E-I-O-U
E-I-O-U
I-O-U
I-O-U?

shit

reflection: on a first kiss

it was as if god had brought us together
and stuck us within a single solitary moment;
closed the door of time   *[pause]*   turned out the light,
and spun the bottle herself

we kissed

we were so far beyond
(for she who is constantly exhausting the possibilities of language)

she just seemed so damn familiar
like we had met eons ago in a past life
where i had been a lonely lily
planted in a crowded garden
and she
she had been this fresh embodiment
of the sweetest rain that i've ever tasted
she was heaven sent, more aptly a divine precipitation
dancing kisses all over my body
nursing me back to health
with just her touch
but we were moving so far beyond that so quickly
so far beyond

childish notes that read:

> *do you like me?*
> *yes or no or maybe (circle one)*

or moments of pleasurable tension
where we played adolescent eye-tag
we were far beyond first introductions,
first phone calls, first dates, and first kisses
we were far beyond lust and love
and that emotion that always seems
to fall somewhere in between the two
we weren't making love

we were making conversation

we were constructing our own language
without the use of standard english
we were making conversation with our eyes
that spoke of past personal insecurities
and future private jokes
only shared between the both of us

i can sense her even undressing
me with her questions
and my overprotective wall built securely
around my pride slipping off my shoulders
to the floor
my insensibility then being lifted over my head
and she cleverly placed compliments
on the centerpiece of my chest
and softly arranged around my bellybutton

i'm thinking thoughts like: *we're moving way too fast*

i certainly can feel her words
slowly traveling across
the terrain of my intellect
and without the use of hands
i can feel the unzipping of my thoughts
in attempt for her to climb
in and through
the window of my pain

i'm thinking thoughts like: *she'll use me*

she was like:
it's just conversation, man, it's just conversation

portrait of a brown girl (on a dream landscape)

I.

and there were two resting on a dream landscape
they both were caught
in the entanglement of late-night conversation
where they would laugh and exchange thoughts
and discuss individual futures
and he had hoped that one day
their paths would cross
and somehow entwine themselves
in blue ribbons and white boxes
and present themselves
in some form of a gift;
in some form of the present
this would be a safe haven
where they would go and share
allegoric hugs and figurative kisses
in the comfort of verbal intimacy

i mean she was clutching me
and touching me
and mentally _____g me
with the words held during our conversation
'til the point that i bled
metaphoric manifestations
of whatever i had been fed
i had been stuffed liked feathered pillows
with past participles that formed
like a congested congregation
that ushered in pronouns

and *mis pronoun ciation*
not to mention the semicolons and conjunctions
that never ever really served
their standard english functions
and i was under the assumption
that she had planted a seed inside of me
producing a garden of language unspoken in proper syntax

                    II.

she though————————
she was beautiful
in every way *[pause]* imaginable
she was brown with a honey tinge
brown like arab sands; cinnamon-tinted
island-scented
she possessed the fragrance of elegance
and i would stare as she would prance
and she would stare as she would prance
and she would tease and offer a momentary glance
which left me staggering in a deepened trance
and all in a moment's time
i would become undone like worn,
decay ed seams
on old hand-me-down jeans
one must understand that this was all
so very new to me and i couldn't decipher
whether or not i was finally
walking in the beauty of my reality
or if i were walking barefoot
on soft-green blades of grass
which were surgically implanted
on a dream landscape to give the illusion
which oftentimes leaves me in a state of confusion

and this is where we had met that fine day
where with her smile, she had warmed me
like benign sun rays that reflect the pride of gays
in oceanic waves of pacific bays
on weekend strolls in the open streets of san francisco

she was the most beautiful portrait
of a brown girl i've ever seen
or
the most beautiful portrait of a brown girl
i've ever dreamed ...
i've ever dreamed ...

sweetest addiction I

can i plant u
grow u
roll u
lick u
smoke u
cvoke u
promote u
even lsd-coat u
then inhale u
in fact
hail u
and name u *"chocolate"*

can i sow u
reap u
lose myself
and yet continue to seek u
can i mentally masturbate u
until i thought-ejaculate u

can i boil u
aluminum-foil u
bake u
cake u
chop u
5th-pocket rock u
bag u
i've got to have u
sell u
inhale u

in fact hail u
and name u something addictive like "*heroine*"

on numbers

she asked if she could be the one

i told her she needn't be
but insisted that she only be half
and i'd be the other

we'd make a whole

and despite the rules and definitions of mathematics,
and although its laws contend that we are two
we knew, in fact, all too well
that we'd had indeed formed to be only but one;

one whole number to be exact

a numeric portrayal of completeness
and nothing would ever be able to…

divide us

wanting to be the air u breathe

i am because u are

i am because u have chosen to give me
the gift of love
i am because u have chosen to give me
the gift of life
breathing life into that which was living
thus giving me new life
and although she was not draped
in old gold and black
or gold and purple
i pledged my love to her
because she was my alpha and my omega
my beginning and my end
my first and my last
she was the perfect embodiment of my futuristic past
i quietly gasped in need of u

but i am wanting
to be so much more
than the one she loves
i am desperately seeking
to be the fresh embodiment
of the air she breathes
i then, being sweetly inhaled,
and being her lone reason for even wanting to exist

because without air   there is no breath
and without breath   there is no life
and without life   there is no u
and without u   there is no i am

because i am simply because u are
and i was thinking
that if you don't want to love me anymore
then i don't want to take another   *breath*

II
amputated feelings

instability

we now age in a day
where feelings are amputated
and replaced with prosthetic apologies

(modern science has failed us in that respect)

one acquainted with feelings of pain

pain came upon me this evening
it crept upon me like old age;
appearing like strands of gray on one's head
unknowingly, without warning or anticipation

it left me gasping for air like one who loves completely

but quickly i collected myself ~
like blown blades of grain do in fields where wind blows
knowing all too well that
winds of trouble are a constant blowing
leaving me toiling in sadness, nestled in the arms of grief

tears soon followed
they came flowing down these cheeks made of cocoa sand
rapidly flowing out of these broken elliptical dams

those damn dams built by years of resentment
that i thought would forever hold

those persistent beavers
would leave an ever fixéd mark upon my heart

dams i swear to all i thought would forever hold
whether it be rain, sleet, or snow;
all too inclusive of pain

faulty craftsmanship

funny how

it's funny how there always is and probably always will be those, those who talk about you not being liberal enough, and those are the ones i find particularly amusing, especially those blacks, though it may not be a laughing matter, who are the ones always talking about others being so foolishly brainwashed, yet they are the same ones who pay their taxes on time and don't drive over 55 and are the same ones who stop for those same damn red octagons that we all do, yet still have the nerve to continuously talk 'bout liberation and 'bout black pride and 'bout black change but won't contribute a single black dollar to black-owned, black-operated businesses in their own black community, aren't even members of their own local chapter of the naacp simply because they refuse to pay dues 'cause they choose to fill other people's pockets by buying the branded news and the latest

sweatshoprobinthehoods*nike*airpairofshoes

and though it may not be a laughing matter
it can be quite funny to recognize
how they are revolutionist when convenient

abusive language

i must be way beyond my past or at least i thought i had been, memory is so oftentimes like that, you spend your whole life attempting to avoid the parts of your past that haunt you like the ghost of hamlet *[pause]* and then you are always having to decipher reality, or if you were just caught in one of those abusive trances you and your therapist had discussed; and all in a moment's time, just the familiar smell of radiator heat, the same radiator heat that would ascend from those vents in that three-room apartment, just that strong sense of familiarity has the ability to open a window of memory and you're forced to climb in and be thwarted back to those abusive times

i must be way beyond my past because i seemed to have forgotten how he would abuse, he used to clenched in his balled fist hurtful verbs and colorful adjectives and slam them against my confidence causing it to become discolored, appearing like some kind of black like some *kind of blue;* he would then proceed to beat me in iambic pentameter causing me to slur my speech like rolling r's with a spanish tongue and he would yell and scream instructing me to speak *eng   lish* properly, but i was just a piece of property and he would oftentimes caution me against using the phone to call the authorities; he would use adjectives to modify my pronouns that made sounds of liberal femininity constantly rein- forcing that i was all alone, and how he was all i that i had; at times like those, i became childlike and longed only to be held in the loving arms of my dad or just someone to hold me, someone to comfort and tell me that it was going to be all right because i've grown sick with purple evenings on moonless nights his love was as conditional as dependent clauses, often times interrupted by offensive language and leaflets on all the causes for spousal abuse in which came these long, momentary pauses; and he being wise enuf to use this time, he would gather in mind all his logical fallacies which enabled him to construct some type of dialogue with self where i was told to speak when spoken to; and me being way too passive, i had no active choice, i had no active voice

i've grown tired of understanding misunderstandings
that would yawn into the morning of my mourning

a part of me had died the night before when he had placed me in brackets, and just the tone of his voice would leave me immobilized and would paralyze my motion while cuffing my wrists together while standing on some seventeenth-century scaffold with a scarlet letter hung around my neck, but somehow, i mustered up the courage to scream "fuck you" with an exclamation point and suddenly remembered a self once whole, a self so distant now so unfamiliar

it's good for you

it's good for you

so i stomached my education
like unwanted peas

it's good for you

so i swallowed the bible whole
to assure my parents that the god they worship now lives in me

i grow older

and for years unbeknownst to me
i had stomached the word and their knowledge
in attempt to avoid sickness
but it was those that had me unwell
and so now i vomit up tasteful deceit in a blue round paper basket
vomits that looks and smells a whole lot like
gospels and capitalism
and the incest of their relationship

my diet now consists of truth
i no longer swallow verses,
nor pray to a god
that leads me into your churches and into your wars
despite the chants of eternal damnation and whispers of:

it's good for you

dancin' with my demons (for ruth otero)

i sometimes
shave my beard,
crease my best pair of slacks,
tuck in my pressed, button-down shirt,
and go dancin' with my demons

despite my christian upbringing

thou reap what thou sow

to be tempted by the serpent's hiss is one,
but another to receive his bite
just as an apple to the soul is bitter,
but to flesh, it is sweet delight

with thy actions thou have pierced the heart of man
thou turned my soul with thy false words
for in truth there is unspeakable joy,
and to mine ears ~ truths have none been heard

why do thee pour salt upon my wound?
why do thee give me vinegar to quench my thirst?
for some unspeakable day, i shall be able to do no more
my flesh shall be confined to this earth

wake up! oh ye sleeper and be thou
quick to think and slow to speak
for if thou hold thy tongue ~ a bad seed will not be sown
and a bad crop thou will not reap

why do thee choose to live a lie?
one which creates hate, and causes pain
and why should we endure this pain?
when thou know the truth can set the captive free
for out there lies much love to gain

the truth i crave
for i shall find the truth before i am buried in my grave!
have it be that if the truth shall kill me
then i ask to let me die an honest death
for if thou seal my death with the truth and then a kiss
thou shall find and taste the words ~ i love you
on my very last bre——

stories like this
(for she who is ten years my senior)

but then there are stories like this and you can't make it out whether or not they are fact or fiction perhaps storied tales peppered with little whites lies that grew to become myths that soon became folklore that, if not for all, then definitely for some, became something of a distant distinctive reality that they would never call their own . . . and that's sad

but no one else understands that

stories like he was this young man attempting to find himself in between each and every crevasse that life had to offer; he would roam around cities asking people had they seen the who he was longing to become or if they could point him in the direction of how to become a self that would be whole, but they kept on pointing him in the direction of churches, colleges, political parties not knowing that he had given up on the intellectualization of christian-dominated political parties' agendas, but then he met her and to be quite honest, she was so close but a distant beauty; she was this matured beauty, when he met her it was like the second coming but for the first time, she was sweet-sweet redemption

but no one else understands that

and then he finds himself waking up at 8:57am on a sunday morning while the creditors have the nerve to call at 9:07am interrupting his thought of her. not sexualizing, but thinking about her. not worried about her, but thinking about her. not even necessarily trying, but just plainly fanatically thinking about her but no one else understands that

it's not that i hadn't given up on love, because believe me, i had; it's just that this is different. it's not that i'm not as cynical or pessimistic about love as you are, it's just that you think you're done before you even begin, but then there are stories like this; and you realize you are in *deep like* because *love* is too strong of a word and *interested* was like 500 yesterdays ago

but no one else understands that

because no else understands or values the thoughts of the house right outside of london, the apartment on 5th avenue, or the beach house in fiji or staying at the carlyle for two weeks on end, high-rise apartments overlooking central park or golf courses, barneys, saks, coach, or burberry (remember burberry), and some may read this poem and think i thought brandon was this sensual, non-materialistic poet, but what they won't understand is that it's not the status or the price, but the inter-intimacies that these products or experiences stood for and the emotional equity you and i invested, and i'll probably have to defend my career over words and terms like wealth, mba, commerce, or phrases like *quality of living*, and they'll criticize me about being inauthentic and vote me to never write another poem, but that'll be okay if i have you, because why write and fancy about it when you already have your stoic beauty; perfection; one's own living masterpiece

but no one else understands that

and as of late, i've begun to question if you even understand that: without you, it's having no one else to watch *love actually* with over and over again and no one to share private jokes about lowering the blinds at 5:38am as the sun begins to come up, with the hope of preserving the night . . . and that's sad but no one else understands that

and if i can't be your forever, i'd even place a bid to be your now or next
five minutes or your next tuesday at 12:00 noon for a matinee or that
cup of coffee in the january of winter that feels as fresh as the new year,
and if i can't be that, then i'll settle for being your next lifetime even if it's
only just a high school crush that you only think about when you visit
your hometown

understand?

growing up

it seems as if things are changing so quickly between us, you don't smile as frequently as you did before; i've even begun to notice that you sometimes on occasion purposely avoid making eye contact and your *good-byes* now sound more like *i'm glad to be going;* perhaps i'm being overly sinister; i have only *bravo* and romantic comedies to blame

but i suppose this is all part of growing up

and i guess it's certainly safe to assume that growing up is quite difficult; i mean vertical growth usually is accompanied by *[pause]* involving growing horizontally, resulting in us or anybody for that matter to experience growing apart; i've even read in one of those grown-up magazines that it's a necessary of division, besides grandmother always warned me about getting too involved at too young of an age, yet her and grandpa been together since they were both 17 and i can't help but think that she tells me this in the casual offering of advice or more so as a word of caution or aging resentment, perhaps a little bit of all three, so i suppose it's best that you go your way and i'll go on mine because we both ought to adhere to the sophisticated american logic and give each other space which is actually something i neither can create nor have the right to apportion, and if my memory serves me correctly, science fact teaches us that there is no sound in space, and we both know that i've always enjoyed science fiction far more than science fact *[pause]* but science fact might justly explain this awkward silence

yes?

but i suppose this is all part of growing up

yet i'm still not so comfortable with silence nor separation seeing that even as of late i've regularly begun to avoid mirrors, trying to evade staring myself in the eyes, afraid that i might see the reasons why you want to leave and have to confront truth, and we all know that confronting truth is as enjoyable as coming to terms with the fact that no matter how many times you comb it, your hair is still nappy, or how many times you suck it in, the scale stills tells you differently, or how many times you smile, your tear-stained pillow tells the world a very different tale of who you really are and that's frightening, but probably not as frightening as the day when you'll say *i'll see you later* and in that moment, we'll both know that it really means *goodbye* and not the afore-mentioned *goodbye*, but *goodbye for good*

but i suppose this is all part of growing up

i promise

i figure if i remain silent long enough
then you'll just forget that i even exist

or at least pretend to

and in keeping with the act of pretending
i'll play the role of the one who's emotionally strong
and keep on make-believing to not be displeased

i promise

breaking

i'm standing outside of the entrance
wanting to leave
longing to leave
but i've grown too
accustomed to not breaking 15-minute breaks

so i return quietly to my office space
where i'm not wanted and underappreciated
until they give me my next break

i'm such a coward

concerning abuse

it's not the concern in my voice, nor the look of concern in my eyes, nor the hint of concern in your voice, but more so, the lack of it in my actions; she would look me in my eyes and i would glare back with sympathetic concern, and there were these nights when i would pretend to ignore, and it wasn't the alarming sound of muffled screams or the americanism to mind one's own business in one's own household, but the stagger in her walk and the artificial excuses that bothered me the most

and this poem apologizes for that

i cannot really say or express that i feel you or feel for you, or i, too, would be wearing *cover girl* in an attempt to shade bruises incurred on purple evenings, and if i really felt you or felt for you, then i, too, would feel the thumping of my body to the floor; i wish i could do more, but i'm not a miracle worker and oftentimes, people want you to perform miracles when all any of us can actually do is our best and then act contrite for things not being different because i'm slowly learning that our best isn't always good enough

and this poem apologizes for that

supply and demand

she asked me why i didn't love her

i gently grabbed onto her attention
and simply told her
she was lacking   *[pause]*   sustenance

she grew angry
and i grew more honest
she began walking away
and i trailed her with the explanation:
that we now age in a day where too many are emotionally malnour-
ished
and reasoned that her supplies weren't quite meeting my demand

(and this had nothing to do with bush taking office and ruining the economy)

appointment

she called her doctor's office but the receptionist asked her to be patient and please hold; and although patience is something that ran in her veins and as far back as the memory of running ancestors, she, too, at times grew tired of *[pause]* patiently holding, but she supposed she shouldn't complain as much as she did

but complaining to her had become almost as habitual as boy meeting girl and boy and girl getting older and older boy loving older girl and older boy penetrating older girl and older girl's stomach growing and older girl thrusting out younger girl and older boy and older girl and younger girl living happily until older girl wakes up one morning and puts her older hand to her older breast and her older hand feels a new lump; hoping it was young but then after a two-year battle, older girl dies from breast cancer; and death told younger girl to hold on because it would soon be her turn because those type of things are hereditary, and she began to grow fearful of mammograms or any other test for that matter, but she thought she'd call to make an appointment anyhow

thank you for holding   *how may i help you?*

on bleaching

and i just can't seem to get by today as i'm sitting there on that bench, that old bench on a cool spring afternoon waiting for a cab when actually all i want to do is to be in new york city in the hustle and bustle of midday perhaps on a 20-minute lunch at my own publishing house while i'm walking down broadway with only $7.50 in my left pocket and a metro pass in my right; but i'm happy, i mean genuinely happy, the kind of happiness you feel when you meet her for the first time, but i'm here in a place where things are not so bad but really have begun to eat away at not only me but my dreams, and there this feeling of self doubt that others have taught me, and now i can't seem to get beyond yesterday's today or tomorrow's yesterdays, so i'm stuck here on this old bench waiting for a newer life to arrive, one that doesn't feel the need to be so afro-centric nor does it feel the need to kiss the ass of those above me because for some strange reason they have the keys and i'm locked out of the doors of opportunity; and despite their claims to be whole-heartedly dedicated to diversity and the advancement of colored people (i've been here too long), i've yet to see not one black dean or vp or someone in a leadership position and they tell me that if i stay around long enough and pay my dues and shine the master's shoes to a nice shine long enough, then perhaps i, too, will be invited to dine at the table with master in the big house; and despite their attempt to brainwash and convince me that'll be next (they still laugh), my hair is still a little too kinky and my lips are still a little too full and i'm a little too tan and my english is a little too articulate for my upbringing in the inner city so i'll either bleach my skin, brush my teeth until they're sparkling white, straighten my hair or continue to sit here on the bench waiting, writing about how i wish things were different

there shall come a time...when...

there shall come a time
when we all must stand alone
there shall come a time
when it seems as if even god is gone

there shall come a time
when no one is there to wipe your tears
there shall come a time
when you are too afraid to even have fears

there shall come a time
when your closest friend becomes the enemy
there shall come a time
when you're in bondage,
and your enemy holds the only key

there shall come a time
when problems seem too hard to bear
there shall come a time
when you will have to endure death's cold stare

wounds turn into scars,
but don't always fade
broken hearts are wounds,
but love too oftentimes seems to be the blade

too often!!!

there shall come a time
when lovers will take separate paths
there shall come a time
when love seems a distant memory in the past

there shall come a time
when "love" seems too much to endure
there shall come a time
when questions arise, but are answered "unsure"

there shall come a time
when true love shall be unmasked
there shall come a time
when "true love" shall be your reward
for all your dutiful tasks

there shall come a time…when…

why do our times differ?
why aren't the ways the same?
people say it is not you, not i, not time, nor destiny
then where shall i cast the blame?

soon thereafter

after engulfing two hard shots of your loving
i returned two of my own
more intoxicating than liquor

as we lay there
entangled in cum-stained sheets
morning softly knocked
on our windowsill

we let in

and were spoon-fed rays of sunlight
and were comforted by our comforter

u rose
i laid
and minutes later
i heard sounds that leaked
from underneath the bathroom door
sounds of you vomiting up choice
in a round blue paper basket

and soon thereafter
your belly began to swell

inconsequential, apologetic forgiveness forgot to remember the importance of human emotion despite tough exteriors...me, too

(for you with apologies)

I.

i dreamt of you last night,
but that has become as familiar as breathing
yet still it pains me to keep my identity a secret
as painful as an infant when teething

just the simple presence of you in a room
sends me muttering like a fool in great embarrassment
palms moistened with nervousness,
voice choked on very words,
and tongue held captive by the fear of resentment

dreams of holding you in my warm embrace ~
of these things...i do have
courage and strong tongue ~ of these things...i have not
and oftentimes i've pondered if i should bind these hopes
and dreams together into a faggot,
and cast them into the furthest sea, anchored by a rock

but quickly i shame the thought
for thou has truly stolen my heart
like a thief in the middle of night
meeting you was likened to a damascus experience,
unexpectedly blurring my sight

i often inquire of what can i say or what can i do to
let you know how much you mean to me

would i have to empty the seven seas,
or even steal and gift-wrap a piece of heaven's beautiful scenery?

or better yet, prepare thee a feast only fit for gods and goddesses
and have you taste the delicious ambrosia
and imbibe the sweetest nectar
or would i have to solemnly swear to be
your steadfast lover and your omnipresent protector?

of all these things,
i know of which no greater length to chase
for thou has truly stolen a piece of my heart ~ gentle thief
yet i sit here and fight one against myself while sick in heart
toiling with my timid actions, nestling in grief

II.

i thought to think of you today ~ and so i did
and suddenly a goofy smile appeared upon my face
the kind of goofy smile you had in sixth grade
when your crush walked passed you in the halls
while you stood there querulously against the lockers
hoping to catch his eye, or perhaps to be caught in the path of his

i thought to call you today ~
but shied from the very thought
with pores flooded with anxiety
perhaps too afraid of twisted tongues
that utter stut-ttering languages
and provoke nervous movements
which only trouble fools in love
for cupid's arrow has certainly found a home
upon the doorstep of my heart, calming all madness
and has also breathed life

into that which was living
removing all clouds
that shadowed my aspirations of gladness

i thought to kiss you today ~
but like wild fire consumes quickly
so does cowardliness
and so i am left to dream of tasting
those lips which are so full of seduction
and taste your skin which is so rich with deep chocolate
just the very thought of your beauty sends me a-flying
unmarred by the state or condition of being grave

i thought to free myself
from this toil and misery of the mind,
and to quickly end the constant struggle
of one against myself
but i can find no sanity in a simple revelation
for love is not simple
and simply
should not be left to simple illustration

III.

i saw you today
and i received chills when touched by your beauty
i smiled in your face and perhaps you knew not that it was i ~
i, who had called into being all those sweet-sounding words
into the form of rhythmic verse,
and had gently slipped them
underneath thou wooden portal
too coward to place them in hand

i saw you again today
and thought to reveal,
but like so many other times…
i shied from the very thought
and hence, waged yet another war one against myself

i saw you a third time today
and was grieved by the very thought
that i had given not a clue
so i stood there
as you read for sure assurance
that it was i ~
i, who stands before you

frightening

i sometimes
wrap my tired body
in linen bed sheets
and rest my thoughts against my pillows
and dream
of your unhappiness

and can envision nothing
being more   *[pause]*   frightening

aging men

an old man is a nasty thing

simply being reduced
to nothing more
than a pot full of bitterness
stirred with excuses

these old aging men are
nothing more than braggarts
who resort to cafés
to chase hard liquor
and dreams
they had forgotten to chase
all the while
unaware that they themselves
are being chased by death

these old men gather
in these pious asylums
to be filled with spirit
and to spill stories of lives once lived

stories that have aged
like bottles of *marquis de villa* wine
aging in spanish cellars

but all are not lost
to the continuous erosion of time
correct…some *do go gently into that good night*
like cowards who remain in barracks in times of war

cowardice action

but few who do battle
battle like men~
like wild men
possessed by something super of a natural being

continuously raging and raging
against the dying of the light
casting aside concerns of caution
and diving once more into the breach ~ for one last fight

applaud these men
these old, aging men

remembering heidi

mother, it's just not fair
she was so young
and grappling with the reality
of her actually being gone
is quite difficult to bear

simply because i'm remembering
the warmth of her smile
and how her spirit was so uplifting
and of late i've grown
not only tired
but angry
from my mood constantly shifting
from sadness to i understand
and people incessantly
telling me to be strong
and seek comforting peace in god
because she's always listening

but i've been strong for years
but i've been strong for months
but i've been strong for weeks
but i've been strong for days
but i've been strong for hours
but i've been strong for minutes
but i've been strong for seconds
been strong for too long

fighting to hold back these tears

i'm tired of resisting

tired of resisting
these tears, because the reality of it is...

is that she died
she being heidi
heidi richardson, to be exact
was called home
well before her time

and she there
and i here
begin shedding so many tears   *[pause]*

kind of like the way
she began shedding so many pounds
in the latter months of her sickness

she had become thinned with shame

she was such a beautiful girl
with milk-toned skin,
dandelion-kinky curls,
american blue eyes,
and patches of freckles that rested
on her shoulder blades in the springtime
accompanied by a birthmark
that resided on the inside of her forearm

she was in fact
very much like you
and i
who just so happened
to meet him

[you'll meet him later]

[smile]

i smile because
i'm remembering
walking into her hospital room
and thinking how ironically beautiful
she looked
and how the shade of blue
in the hospital gown matched so perfectly
with the shade of blue held in her eyes

and i   *[pause]*
probably like you   *[pause]*
and like you   *[pause]*

would hope
the blue was more symbolic
of free blue skies
juxtaposed against stilled white clouds
instead of her actually basking in the blues
of her own shame

did i forget to tell you that she was thinning with shame?

and i don't know
if you have ever seen a person
dwindle and fade
right in front of your own eyes

but i have

she was fading like…like…like…
innocence
she was fading like
innocence
gripped by time,
strangled by age,
and infected by the human condition

she was fading like…like…like…
long-distance relationships
with sprint pcs cell-phone service
our signals began fading
and we couldn't connect
if we paid roaming charges

she was drifting closer to her
and further from me

[her being god and me being i]

i angered at her and in return
she showed me love
i then stood confused and angered
crying
she began to comfort
and i suddenly understood
theorems of what exactly love is

and had a clear innerstanding
of her purpose
and i was able to let go
of all the hate bottled inside me
that i had for him

[him being ralph]

ralph being the guy who infected heidi with it

[it being aids]

and him dying slowly
could only offer
"i'm sorry, heidi, i should've told you"

she replied, "no, i'm sorry, ralph,
i should've known better,
i just don't understand why you didn't tell me."

he muttered, "it just feels better that way,
i thought it would be more intimate."

she cried out,
"what being more intimate, the both of us sick and dying?"

he was frozen silent

and i, now being here
she now being up there *(if there even exists a place)*
ralph now being down there *(i'm more hopeful)*
thinking
i'm thinking that perhaps...

if he could've told her that he was sick
then she might still be here

and i probably wouldn't have had to skip heidi's funeral

it's usually

it's usually in the still of a cold wintry evening or more so late nights when i am waiting for the 11:01 train to arrive from grand central that i begin to...and never finish putting my life in order

it's usually then that i imagine a future when all my bills are all paid up: i'll have a big screen color tv (plasma, if i save) carpeting from srvatite, and a nicely rolled veggie wrap that doesn't fall apart when you lift it, with all the toppings of lettuce, tomato, onions, pickles, vinegar, and extra oregano

boarded the train. i'm sitting there imagining a happier time when one doesn't have concerns about parents' low-income, high-cholesterol or high-blood pressure, or rent and car payments, or student loans or girl-friend's father's christian-ignorance, which has probably had some psychological affect on your girlfriend's psyche, explaining just why she finds so much comfort in you

it's usually the sound of water silently dropping from the station's over-head passageway off in the near distance that makes one think that there is peace in this world; it makes one think that perhaps there is safe inter-national travel and that bullied kids will not kill those bullies because bullies won't exist if there is peace, and people wouldn't have to send flowers or have flags raised at half mast if we didn't incite such evil deeds, because as clear as nikki giovanni put it "those are desperate acts commit-ted by desperate people" and sometimes when i feel cornered, closed off to the world, trapped, i suppose by even some definition, desperate, i if not sympathize, then at least understand the persons who do commit desperate acts like going on shooting sprees, airplane hijackings, suicide bombings, or budget cuts—perhaps i've said too much

but when the bills are due and the lights are cut off and you have candles and no matches because you dropped them in the water that came from the overflowed toilet because the superintendent doesn't believe in making night calls, and you feel kind of trapped, kind of desperate and all that i'm saying is that desperate people think desperate thoughts that translate into desperate actions resulting in desperation

i know life is cyclical but let us stop this

i, too

i, too, know a thing or two about loneliness
i've ridden facing backwards on trains
with book bags, umbrellas, and other authors
as my only companions

believe me

i, too, have sat there with the crest of my forehead
pressed up against the window of inner pain
hopelessly staring out at passing cities
and the blurred faces of familiar strangers
desperately in search of hands that i can trust
perhaps hands that i can even someday call my own

believe me

i, too, have felt like
a pebble caught in the sole of society
slowly being dragged along the summer's burning pavement

believe me

i, too, have felt like
pulling the earth over me
and finding the sweet salvation
that lies in the eternal solitude of death

reflection: on childhood

remembering as a child
nothing being more interesting
than meeting a stranger
nothing being more comforting
than receiving the chill from a familiar pillow
and lying in the warmth of one's own bed

remembering as a child
nothing being more enjoyable
than having sleepovers
nothing being more saddening
than watching friends and neighbors move

remembering as a child
nothing being more painful
than a scraped knee
nothing being more frustrating
than learning how to tie your own shoelaces

remembering as a child
nothing being more heartbreaking
than the loss of an uncle
nothing being more confusing
than inoperable cancer and the definition of terminal illness

remembering as a child
nothing being more intriguing
than death itself, and the attending of funerals
nothing being more valuable

than family

remembering as a child
nothing being more secure
than resting on the shoulders of a father
nothing being more unstable than...
as i remember as a child
nothing seemed so unstable

remembering as a child
nothing being more disappointing
than the fact that we all were living in *projects*
that seemed unfinished by the government
nothing being more challenging
than those youthful years
when i was searching for a way out

remembering as a child
nothing being more persistent than bill collectors
(lights had been turned off, phone disconnected)
nothing being more constant
than the sight of liquor stores on every corner

remembering as a child
nothing being more agonizing
than seeing the emptiness that lay in my mother's eyes
nothing being rougher
than the callused hands of a working father

remembering as a child
nothing being more complex
than the reasoning behind the question:
if god is omnipresent, then where does evil exist?
nothing being more essential

than two older brothers who continuously
raised the bar, as opposed to just sitting in one

remembering as a child
nothing being more needed
than a listening ear and a shoulder to cry on
nothing being more consoling
than words volleyed during
intimate conversations held between friends

remembering as a child
nothing being more dividing...
than time, and simply just growing up
nothing being more wrong
than hating differences

remembering as a child
nothing being more hurtful
than the day i was called a *nigger* on the playground
nothing being harsher
than the reality of racism...my first, not my only encounter

remembering as a child
nothing being more distant
than adulthood
nothing being more troublesome
than simply remembering as a child

unperfectly quilted

she's a perfect fit to my puzzle
she rejects me like all the others
and although amputated feelings and emotional scars
are the hardest to heal
principally because most convenient stores
don't sell type of healing balm i'm in need of

how convenient?

but there are lessons to be learned
and experiences to be treasured
so although we journey on separately
my heartbeat continues to speed up
when i begin to stitch even the simplest
thought of you

besides i can certainly appreciate
the timeless, divinely inspired art of consistency
despite it's curse

and although you being perfectly interwoven
into the fabric of my life
time had worn it thin
and the relationship seemingly began to fall apart at the seams
the bond weakening through argument and regrettable action

although a perfect addition
she being a quilted moment of a departed past
distinctly following a pattern
mother had taught

but that i soon forgot

so i stood there with needles of reason
and thread of little understanding...

attempting

but had only my ignorance to blame

and when the time came
as time always does come
in its own time...
i was helpless

i mean...

completely, utterly, humanly, fatefully helpless
when our relationship began to unravel at the seams

the american dream

i oftentimes dream of a happier me, one that doesn't frown as much, one that doesn't become as angered at news reports as frequently or curse when young people don't hold the door for me or when pop music doesn't seem relevant to my life anymore *(as if it did, i being an african-american male and all)* or when music doesn't make sense to me anymore, but i suppose that this is all part of the aging process; it's always disheartening when you try so very hard to connect with a culture, a people, generation, or even the fashions of a younger era hoping to avoid responsibility but soon realizing all is too late, for those days are gone

just wishing for a time when you didn't have to keep up appearances or yes your boss to death, a time when you didn't depend so heavily on coffee in the morning or something, more or less anything, to clog your arteries in the afternoon and the dread of traffic on your commute home from your reward, from your investment that cost you or someone else you know anywhere from $80,000–$135,000 for a bachelor's degree

and in the midst of your life, even in the midst of reading this poem, you feel the need to succeed far beyond the point in your life at which you are currently at now, but can't seem to muster the courage to stop getting out of line or out of the routine of catching the bus to catch the train only to catch the bus to then pay for a cab, only to catch the train and catch yet another cab home because you have obligations and you, you, you, and very much like you who hadn't even thought to pick up this poem are thinking i would like to stop sleep walking through life, but you see the rent runs up against the car note up against the stafford college loans up against the groceries up against the phone bills up against the need to survive

and when you think you have somehow mustered up enough courage
and energy to stop sleepwalking through your life

the government wakes you up and says,

"welcome to the american dream."

re: memory

i never really would've expected it
to turn out the way it has
(my life that is)
i don't want to remember
being surrounded as a child
by pawn shops and liquor stores

it's actually quite difficult
(no, really, it is)
to accept the fact that we slept
ten people to a two-bedroom apartment
in those ridgegate projects
i was once asked the question
"why do they call it the 'projects' anyway?"
are we some type of governmental experiment?

it's actually quite difficult
to *re   member*
receiving thanksgiving and christmas
gift baskets from the church   *[pause]*
we would've starved

it has always been
very heartrending to remember
living five people to a single
motel room for weeks
when all of your belongings
are packed in your parents'
'73 station wagon in sardine fashion
and all that you have

is held between those car doors

it's very emotionally trying
to *re   collect*
parts of my past and somehow,
in some lethargic way
attempt to piece together
the fragmented moments of enjoyment
i experienced in my collegiate years
where i played football in exchange
for some grade-A, euro-centric,
white-male dominant, wholly misogynistic,
catholic, liberal arts education
perhaps i am being way too critical
but i feel intellectually malnourished
even though i've been stuffed
like feathered pillows
with storied lies about my history

(a special thanks goes to my guidance counselor)

two roads diverged
i took the one less traveled by,
and that has made all the difference
[pause]   in me
for my journey
has made me indifferent,
bitter, and hateful of self
more so than i had ever anticipated
and though i grow weary
i must *re   member*
that *i've promises to keep,*
and miles to go before i sleep

it's very distressing to *re   member*
my uncle smoking four packs
of marlboros a day
and then dying of some type
of inoperable lung cancer   *[pause]*
he's been dead for some time now;
126,213,120 seconds...and counting
i become dazed with memories

he's cheated me out of so much of our future
he's cheated me out of so much happiness

it's very painful to *re   member*
feeling intellectually inferior
every time i raised my hand
in a classroom   *[pause]*
some say that it may be
my own insecurities
that they had broken into
and had somehow stolen
my confidential records
on how to be self-confident   *[pause]*

but it has always felt
as if the board of education
has actually grown bored
with the education of my people;
our children are being mentally molested
and culturally raped
in these schools that are named
after these grand ol' presidents
who were nothing more
than racist pedophiles, self-absorbed,
slaveholding individuals

but i can certainly understand
if you do not wish to *re   member*
those parts of america's history

cause even i at times
i don't want to *re   member*
i don't want to *re   member*
living in poverty
i don't want to *re   member*
going hungry or being cold
i don't want to *re   member*
sounds of gunshots
i don't want to *re   member*
sneakers hanging from power lines
i don't want to *re   member*
the smell of alcohol
i don't want to *re   member*
doo-rags, timberland boots,
air jordans, starter jackets, and gold chains
i don't want to *re   member*
being told i was too dark
i don't want to *re   member*
words like "nigger"
i don't want to *re   member*
being *[looooooong pause]*   black
i don't want to *re   member*
being

*this has been a brief moment in black history paid for by your attention. thank you.

depression
(for kirk nugent, with apologies)

i, too, no longer write about depression   *[pause]*

i live it

friendship
(honesty with few apologies)

a friend is nothing more
than a well-painted picture
on a fictitious canvas
reflecting a falsehood
misplaced in reality
carefully hung on the walls
in the gallery of my insecurities
with the hope of being mistaken
or appreciated for true or authentic art
friendship is faith without religion

a friend is this and so much more…

a friend is an imposter compiled solely
of good intentions
void of any real action
who masquerades around
in garments of truth
speaking fiery words of compassion
mother should have named you Claudius
pouring in mine ear
the poison of false admiration
and singing aloud
chords of duplicitous praise
with the hope of stirring emotion
while presenting an illusory sense
of camaraderie and of brotherhood
friendship is a cancer without healing

a friend is this and so much more…

a friend is an oppressor of childhood dreams,
adolescent aspirations and adulthood realities
and can most aptly be identified
by it's use of phrases like
"oh, i'm sorry," and "i'm just,"
which holistically come together
to formulate my all-time favorite phrase:

*"i'm sorry and i wish i could
help you but i'm just doing my job"*

friendship is a most terrible thing
friends are these things and nothing more   *[period]*

this poem hates...too

it's like you go to school because you really think it is important to get educated and stay current with intellectualism so that you can lead a better quality of life when you get older, but as you get older, you actually wake up a little bit behind the academic curb, pretty much they way you were before you went off to school and then think that maybe something is wrong with the whole fucking thing and you can't exactly put your finger on it, but you think it has something to do with the elitist group in this country or the bush family (i'm so redundant) or the fact that you are a black male in america and just how unpopular that is unless you run really fast or jump very high or defame yourself and your counterpart while hopping around on a stage or in a club or on BET (oh, god...BET), or on mtv's trl, just as long as you are hopping around with gold chains and improper grammar, but you can't put your finger on it, but then think that the elitist group or bush family (there i go again) or white people in general are sending young black and brown boys and girls off to school, drowning them in debt and then not hiring them, despite the fact that kwame sat next to kimberly in the same managerial economics class and did substantially better, yet she's got a job paying $45,500 a year while he's been on a job search for 18 months while he works at wal-mart (and we've all read the reports on wal-mart and how they treat their employees) or perhaps it's shamar who is doing the graveyard security shift for $9.80/hr, $11.40/hr on weekends while looking out for people with last names he can't even pronounce so that they feel safer and more secure and so that orange doesn't go to red or yellow or you know what i mean, but i can't put my finger on why white people marginalize us, whether it's for sport or fun or whatever the reason, it is that people in power marginalize other powerless people which is not for passion or financial gain...i think i've stumble on to something so you very much, like i, wish you could go back to before you were educated when all you knew was happiness and didn't yet understand poverty

but mostly what bothers you is that you begin to understand rage and pure hatred and suddenly 9/11 doesn't seem so inconceivable (perhaps i've said too much), and there usually comes out of the black and blue of shitty circumstances, a certain level of clarity to why people go crazy or overdose on meds, why men drink to escape and women fuck to feel necessary, why people are as crotchety and irritable as they are because at this point you kind of get the notion that there are fathers who do actually in real life i mean i'm talking real people with real diseases minus the lights and camera and a great actor of our time like denzel, who do in fact get denied treatment for their little boy's leukemia or heart transplant because he got laid off 3 months ago due to his job being outsourced to india, and it's not that i have anything against india or that company in particular but it's just that the father could've used the job right now so that his son could receive treatments, and despite his and his family attempt to collect money from the community and church people and from whomever you, too, would collect money from if you found out someone you loved was dying, but it never seems to be enough for the hospital board of trustees, so then when the boy dies and the father walks into the health provider's office and shoots everybody on that floor you don't feel sadness but more-so empathetic, since nobody wanted to listen to him when he was begging and pleading for a chance at saving his little boy's life, so yes i do understand why people steal things as big as airplanes and fly them into buildings or why people overdose on things as a small as pills, so it's not really about the logic behind it because as clear as i see, logic went out the window a long time ago as some people do when other people stop listening to them, but the news reporter and the newspaper writer will never write or report that they deserved it because all the father was asking for was for someone to pay attention to his family, and all they were asking for was for someone to give them a chance to present their side of the answer but it's like no one ever understands that, and when no one is listening they just go on feeling as if they don't matter and this poem recognizes that and this poem will not whine because a whine is too adolescent and a whimper is too weak and a scream is too...well...logical so this poem sighs and wishes things were better and that things didn't have to be like this

this poem hates, too

III

prosthetic apologies

a poem: written in blank verse

"

"

thought (on a gift)
(for my hominess)

you are my perfect now
i am hoping to unwrap forever

i've decided

i've decided to stay for the simple reasons that
i know the pain of leaving
and understand all too well
the hurt that gnaws away at one's existence
when you look at someone you used to love

someone you now want to love
someone you now need to love
but know now that you can't love

either because your selfish pride has decided against it
or perhaps it's just circumstance, fate,
or as so many christians categorize "*all in god's plan*"
and despite your atheist point of view
the latter is starting to kind of make sense

nonetheless you're sitting there alone
attempting to understand why you left in the first place
quietly thinking to yourself:

if only i'd decided to *un   decide* what i've decided
i would be still be in her arms
nestling in compromised reassurance
traveling toward ritualistic vows and normalcy

while daily continuing to bargain away my freedoms

experiencing womanhood

i want to experience womanhood
so that i wouldn't have to be such a fucking guy

i want to experience womanhood

so that i can experience intimacy, compassion, and even sensitivity
so that sexism becomes something i've actually experienced rather
than heard or read about

i want to experience womanhood

so that i wouldn't have to walk around with my chest out
and my shoulder back or my pants slightly sagging
while my left hand's on my jock and my right hand's covering my
mouth posing to be the next b-boy talking about:

yo, son, did you see the chic ass?

boys…will be boys
simple boys who grew to men
and men are generally boys
who grew up
but not out of
the mentality of boyhood
so i'd rather experience womanhood

i want to experience womanhood

so that if ever our relationship

seemingly begins to unravel at the seams
you wouldn't fear knowing that
grandmother had been a seamstress for years
and teaching granddaughters how to sew
is something that grandmothers just do

so that i can actually admit
that i, too, need arms of care
to surround me when i feel like a pebble
caught in the sole of society
being slowly dragged along the pavement
so that i can admit that touch is needed
and that kissing is intimate
and that sex is actually a sharing of one's soul with another
and so that i wouldn't have to pretend to not be
romantically in love with watching romantic comedies

i want to experience womanhood

so that i can watch shows like *the view*
and stations like *oxygen* and actually enjoy *lifetime* movies
even when male friends enter the room
so that i can grow my nails
as long as men's erections
and paint them the color of rainbows
without anyone holding my sexual orientation in question

so that i can experience children breaking me open
experiencing the sensation of growing and nurturing a life in the
placenta of motherhood

i want to experience womanhood

so that i can cook, clean, and perform 3-minute quickies

i want to experience womanhood

so that i can watch *barney, dora the explorer,*
and sponge bob squarepants
attend *pta* meetings, drive mini-vans,
and be officially declared a soccer mom

i want to experience womanhood

so that i can be hollered at and whistled at
i wanna be called *mami,* and *shorty,* and *bitch*
and even told to *suck a dick* with some sincerity
boys' locker room talk is so inoffensive

i want to experience womanhood

so that my tits can have a million and one
conversations with men's eyes

i want to experience womanhood

so that i can be molested by inebriated strangers
or drunken fools at family reunions
or told how beautiful my ass looks
when i stroll through the cubical maze at my office job
where i work for 6 or 7 thousand less than my male counterparts
all the while having to put up with sexual harassment on daily basis
coming home feeling void of any real success

i want to experience womanhood

so that terms like spousal abuse and sexual harassment
are realities and not just 30-second sound bytes

on the 6 or 10 o'clock news
that only happen in other people's houses
so that i can live the storied lives of *girls interrupted*

while they ask me to ignore
the upset stomachs, the dizziness,
the nervousness, and the fatigue

i want to experience womanhood

so that i can feel men's eyes rolling in between my thighs
in search of some pu   litzer   *[pussy]*   prize all the while
never quite *real eyesing*
that these *real eyes* of a woman can see through
the false *real ities* that men create
all this while exposing the *real ities*
that men spur during conversations
of how much they love women and their femininity

i want to experience womanhood

so that i can understand that a kiss
on the first date with a closed mouth
is not an invitation for men to break open
into my *in   securities* while breaking
through the hymen of my innocence
years later group circles would encompass
my own *in   securities* and the *in   securities*
of other women all the while being encircled
by conversations about nights of tear-stained pillows
and blood-stained sheets   *[pause]*   revisited
rape never sounded so horrific
until i read my own newspaper clipping

i want to experience womanhood

so that i can
finally gain an understanding of *rape*
finally un comprehend *abortions*
and unmake sense of the *morning after pill*
finally fully ungrasp the concept behind *birth control*
and come to terms with reoccurring *pregnancy scares*

i want to experience womanhood

so that i can be as strong as you
as courageous as you
as open as you can be at times
i want to smile as you do…you smile as if the sun is never to set

i want to experience womanhood

so that for once i can be blindly in love with someone
as only a woman can
i'm talking about that:
excuse me, miss, i don't mean to rude, impolite, ill-mannered, or
uncouth but your man and i's connection is far more important than
some petty catfight and the reason why i need to be with him certainly
outweigh the reasons why he should stay with you kind of love
i'm talking about that totally inconvenient love
that only women experience

i want to experience womanhood

so that i can understand...
so that i can be unafraid
to confront my own manhood

i want to experience womanhood

so that i wouldn't have to be such a   *[fucking]*   guy

i want to experience womanhood

so that i wouln't have to be such a   *[fucking]*   guy

divine purpose

someone asked us if we were in love
we both silently chuckled
i explained that this had very little
to do with us, choice, or love

and everything to do with divine purpose

dad

i kind of like the way
or can certainly appreciate
how we used to always just get by
the way we'd exchange pocket change
day to day, week to week, and year to year
in order to get exactly what we needed

like *"here you go, son,*
i've got three dollars in quarters
and if you've got two dollars in dimes and nickles
then you'll be able to catch the train back to school
because the car is not starting tonight
and i know you have class in the morning"

so i guess even i have to admit that,

although it's been kind of rough with you
not being able to work these last couple of years
i don't mind it one bit
and what i've always found strikingly interesting is,
is that not much has changed of late

not the genuine affection in your love
not the sincerity held in your laughter,
nor the luster in your smile

and for those reasons alone
i know i'm eternally grateful to be able to call you *dad*

pleasure

i suppose to some, pleasure would be
defined as a source of delight,
frivolous amusement,
or even some grand sensual gratification

but even i know better

it could quite possibly be a principle
when an individual's behavior
has the tendency to be directed toward
immediate satisfaction of instinctual drives
or the modus operandi
of immediate relief from pain or discomfort

but even i know better

it may well conceivably be a principle
we all learned of in the mid-80s
when guys sported
high-tops faded with the zigzag parts
and girls were dancing
draped in leotards, and loud, colorful scrunchy socks
and stonewashed jean jackets

but even i know better

and you said those days were fresh
and i kind of agreed
and you said those days were full of pleasure

i wanted to agree

but even i know better

i know better
only because one day you spoke to me
and subsequently that year you touched me
and later on that decade you held me
and while you held me
you began loving me
and i learned that pleasure cannot be defined
by anyone or anything other than your love...

'cause even i know there is no pleasure outside of...

your love

god

even in euro-marxism
god, to most, is considered to be a he,
but i know god personally
and i can assure you that god is a she
and not a he at all
in fact, she sometimes lets me call her me

she birthed creation
she is no virgin queen,
but the fertile vessel of sexuality and creativity
regarded as both sacred and central

yes?

joy II

i've grown bitter with happiness;
happiness is so temporal

so i've begun my journey in a desperate search for joy
that unspeakable joy that mother and pastor
had always spoke about on early sunday mornings

heroes

in mythology and legends, a hero is defined as a man, often of divine ancestry, who is endowed with great courage and strength, celebrated for his bold exploits, and favored by the gods or categorized as a person noted for feats of courage or nobility of purpose, especially one who has risked or sacrificed his or her life, and there certainly could be made a case for those fearless new york city firefighters and policemen and policewomen who ran into those burning buildings on 9/11; i could only imagine, no to be quite honest, no i can't, although i wish i could grasp an understanding of what makes humans commit such admirable acts of bravery when they don't necessarily have to but feel the need to and somehow muster the courage inside of themselves to ignore the rationale of the increased possibility of death since science fact tells them if they go inside a burning building, then their life expectancy will be instantly cut in half, so i suppose that we should tip our hats or offer a curtsey for those brave men and women, applaud them and call them the most heroic heroes, not only for the act, but for the ignoring of american logic that tells individuals to worry about self and self only, so i guess we should call them heroes or at least write a letter to congress asking them to recognize them annually

and i thought we ought to have a conversation about this

i've even once read that heroes are not necessarily those persons with supernatural, cosmic power who have the ability to leap a building in a single bound or travel at the speed of a bullet, but more so those individuals who are not brave all the time, just when it counts, but i'm sure if we all could pause and pull ourselves away from the television or just turn down the radio ignoring rush limbaugh's ignorant commentary and all those other self-absorbed republicans on the right, then take no notice of the logic embedded in americanism that tells us to sit in our individual homes or apartments we can barely rent and condos we rent but can't really afford, then we would be able to find heroes in our own communities, because heroes of our day are ordinary people who do extra-ordinary things like tip a cab driver so that he can pay for his child's medical co-pay or a winter coat that might have prevented this particular doctor visit or mentor a young person or teach child how to make grits (and not that instant stuff) because anybody who's anybody with an ounce of sense knows that grits are a timely process that requires attention because you must stir it consistently, add a pinch of salt, put just enough butter with a couple dashes of sugar or a couple slivers of country cheddar cheese, and if you're really adventurous, then you'll mix it with scrambled eggs

and this poem seeks to acknowledge those individuals

you see the brunt of it is that people of the 20th and 21st century have not only put their lives on the line but their sanity, dignity, and sanctity with the hope of a recovered tomorrow; one that doesn't kill nearly as much, one that isn't so concerned with rights to carry a hand gun, one that doesn't tell sick and dying people that they will not authorize a treatment or an operation because he/she doesn't have the required coverage to perpetuate the game of the law that only helps and permits healthcare provider to provide only for those who can purchase the equipment so that the game can go on in style

and that's very disturbing so i thought we ought to talk about it today

and if that's not heroic enough, then perhaps we ought to put down our webster's and oxford dictionaries and begin to redefine not only a word but a time

re: when i grow up
(for samirah umarah eshe)

when i grow up

i want to be a poet

i want to be that everfly cornerman,
pusherman poet pumping poetic smack
in and throughout your veins
having you all already addicted to my diction
without the least bit of suspicion
of whether or not the shit that i'm spittin'
is real or just some fairytale fiction

i want to be a poet

i want to verbally intoxicate you
mentally thought-rape you
impregnate u
with this poetry

i want to be a poet

because i fuck nouns for freedoms
and trick out verbs on the *reg*
i've had **ménage à trois** with pronouns and adverbs
and even gave iambic pentameter head
i told y'all

i want to be a poet

4 months (nadia-aryelle)

when i hold her
i noticed she is scented
with the fragrance of her mother's neck   *[pause]*

i hold her close

inhaled

and for that lone reason
i know to call her mine

her
(for a beautiful mind)

i've always thought the circumstances
underneath which we met to be most peculiar
for reasons that
you were from westport
and i was from waterbury
and i really can't stand modernized remakes
of good theater like *west side story*
and even more oddly
you were supposed to be in london
studying abroad for a semester
and i...

to be quite honest...wasn't looking
but it was one of those *forces of nature* things
when i, by chance, looked over to the left
and you glanced up momentarily to the right
and we just sat stilled in a brief moment
of intimate silence
where we exchanged goofy grins

and later
phone numbers, pleasurable touches, extended kisses
political, philosophical, and religious viewpoints,
and past personal histories

and if todays were yesterdays
there's no doubt i'd miss you tomorrow and tomorrow and tomorrow

forever

spirituality

desiring to no longer walk after the flesh,
but after the spirit
and growing tired of itching and scratching
i quietly ripped off my skin
and bathed in vinegar
in search of some moral happiness

i am renouncing this world
in the pursuit of the spiritual world

Brandon M. Graham

it seems rather odd (that i would)

i want to hold onto past pain
in the palm of my future's happiness
as a reminder that the present
is actually a gift in and of itself

that summer

it's not that i mind it much but rather that she was so young and you were working so hard at becoming accustomed to this newly found motherhood, and it just bothered me to see you hiding the fatigue in your eyes behind the charm in your smile so well, and rather than viewing your eyes as windows, i saw yours as mirrors reflecting the fatigue in mine; no matter my argument but to be quite honest, it really wasn't the early morning rise, the summer heat, nor the hills that surrounded your house, what was most disturbing to me was that i remember as a child growing up that christians weren't supposed to harbor unforgiveness in their hearts (especially pastors, and believe me i do recognize that he was more than a pastor and that he may be acting out of humanity or more directly out of fatherhood but as a clergyman, one shoulders a certain level of responsibility and that's all i'm saying) and i can remember mrs. sargent in sunday school class reading from matthew saying we all were supposed to give food to those who hunger and offer water to those who thirst and provide shelter for those who had none, i mean weren't we? but your father would just look on with a auspicious grin on his face while we would, despite the summer heat, scrounge together three dollars and ten cents mostly compiled of dimes and nickels and would get 2 fudge rounds, 2 small bags of doritos (one original, one ranch), 4 quarter-waters, 2 packs of juicy-fruit, 5 lollipops, 1 orange sunkist chew and hide in the shade of a few branches, mixing formula for her and not once did we ask why things had to be the way they were, we just kind of dealt with it

that summer

loving u more
(for she who is constantly exhausting the possibilities)

i love u...

more than circumstances
more than comfort zones
more than luxuries

i simply love u more...

more than personal freedoms
more than previous commitments
more than contractual agreements

more than lonely walks uphill
more than early morning bus transfers
more than inflated cab fares
more than cold train rides
more than on-time airplane flights

more than impatience
(which inevitably)
leads to late night arguments
and early morning apologies
more than jealousy
more than disagreements
more than confrontations

i simply love u more...

more than late night conversations
on the telephone that end with
"hang up, no u hang up first"

more than moments of intimate silence shared between us

i simply love u more...

more than childhood fears
more than adolescent worries
more than middle-age insecurities

more than religious yolks
(besides, you like your eggs scrambled and i like mine over-easy)
more than a mother's wisdom
more than a father's inhibition
more than a best friend's quarrel

i love u...

more than the distance shared between us
more than the favorable advice of peers
who say long distance relationships never work out

more than those who said no when we said yes

and to be quite honest
i'm not really certain just how
or particularly why
we, in fact, did say yes
i'm just kinda glad we did

i love u...

more than possibility

i love u...

simply because u saved me
and that's not a theological statement

i love u...

because one day u woke up
and walked through the doors of room 234E
deciding that i would love u

i love u...

more simply because
u embodied the concept of less
and   *[pause]*   became a contradiction
the result being that oftentimes
u are much more...much more than i can handle

bluntly spoken:

i love u more than my own salvation   *[period]*

i miss
(for my hominess)

the sight of tears
streaming down your right cheek
the taste of salty tear residue
residing on the upper crest
of your lip
whenever you have to leave

and we have to say our goodbyes

whenever you come
whether it's for 3 or 5 days

or 3 or 5 minutes

i miss

caressing the softness your earlobes
and playfully planting kisses on your cheeks
or attending matinees and holding pinkies
sitting on the same side of the booth when dining
and although some may comment
and say things like, "ahh, how cute"
they'll really never quite understand the depths of this

they'll really never quite understand
why third-world debt
9/11 hearings
political conventions and presidential elections
alaska's 7.3 percent unemployment rate

the aids epidemic in africa
the fact that 855,000,000 *poeple our illiteirate*
the rapid growth of world hunger
2.1 millions being imprisoned
orange or red terror alerts
suicidal bombings
don't seem to matter much to me

seemingly they can't grasp why these things aren't so disconcerting
in a time when almost all seems so uncertain and so unsure

they'll never understand why none of that matters when i'm with you

to mother: on her birthday in her fiftieth year

nearly one score ago
i came to you in thrashing pain
you held me in my innocence
all the while ushering praise toward heaven
for my very existence
you have shown me love;
love that clasped firmly to my tongue
inhibiting it from uttering any intelligible sound
for rationale of why, how, or where from this endless flow
of love had sprung from

let today be a reflection of 50 years of happiness
in spite of financial struggles, family toil, and maternal grief
this day i would urge you to laugh in the face of divorce
and hurriedly clench tightly to the uncertainty of a second spring
~ and simply smile
smile, knowing that you have been an honorable servant
to us all of very great worth
and i say that with a humble tongue

reflect and recall how you have bathed me in my nakedness
with abundant love, dried me with compassion and concern,
and powdered me with your vast knowledge
on how to live a life that would be approved by your god
thus more, you have cleansed my soul with thou biblical verse
and have draped me in christian commitment
you have etched the teachings of your god upon my heart
and have bound them around my neck
and inscribed them upon the tablet of my heart
that i might not sin against

i have grown tired of watching you return home
from these modernized cotton fields
which demand long hours and render only short pay
my heart has begun palpitating from grief
yet i feel handcuffed by extenuating circumstances
which plague my thoughts daily
so i choose to live life for nothing more than second chances
and oftentimes, i have caught you in many a deep trance
with thoughts of how, when, where from...
hung upon your face with that empty stare
i, too, grew frustrated from seeing you
barely meet your needs all the while having none or very little
of what that little girl had always longed for
if it wasn't a big mansion
would you settle for a big rest?
a endless stretch of time
in which you could regain your youth
and flip the pages of that book of truth
that has been a comforter in times when comfort was needed
you wouldn't have to answer any phone calls
or repetitive questions from those who surround you
you would lie so ever gently in a bed of tulips
blanketed by the love of a husband

patience!!!

for god has granted you favor
her hand has been firmly pressed upon thou life
and has been the cloud by day and the fire in the midnight hour
at times, i see that little girl that still thrives inside of you ~
i want to give her "her wants"
once again i say patience ~ patience my dear
if it is not too much trouble,

i would ask that you listen without interrupted thought
for i wish to thank you

thank you,
for sitting by my bedside in the darkest hour
placing cold rags, prayers full of fire upon my brow
and patiently waiting for my fever to break

thank you,
for wiping my nose when sneezing
and for enabling me to continue breathing
by placing vicks vapor rub on my body
when my chest was wheezing

thank you,
for the prayers to a familiar but unseen god
because i, too, have felt her hand pressed upon my life
and for the constant reminder that she loves me

thank you,
for cups of tea softly stirred
with lemon and a pinch of sugar
for miracles on christmas,
and for birthdays that made me feel
as if god had birthed that day for me alone
for comforting words of praise when in despair
and for humbling scripture when my id grew too large

thank you,
for understanding my adolescence
far better than any book written on how to...

i sing a hymn of much deserved praise
for all the loads of laundry,

loads of aggravation placed upon thou back
for rooms, well-lit by candles when
there wasn't enough currency to produce electric currents
believe me ~ the times when you went to pay the phone
to make arrangements when the phone had been cut off
do not go unnoticed

thank you

just callin'

i desperately want to be
the much needed phone call
in the green of morning
that awakens u
to the dawning of a new day

i want to alarm u
with the sound
of a telephone ringing
i can envision u awaking;
stumbling over dreams
in an attempt
to catch my call

"hello," in a raspy voice

"i know it's kind of early
and you are probably thinkin',
hell, even i'm thinkin',
who would think to call so early
not even thinkin'
that perhaps you were asleep
and couldn't it wait 'til later

but it's just that...

i was thinkin' that maybe
if i waited 'til later
that u and i
would both be tortured

by the thought
that we hadn't spoken
to each other all day
so i was just thinkin' bout
all the beautiful thoughts
that encamp around my mind
whenever i begin
to create even the simplest thought
of thinking 'bout you
so i thought to call

not even thinking about the time.

respect

believe me when i tell you it's not that i don't respect you because i do, to be quite honest i sometimes play aretha franklin and fall asleep thinkin' of you and awake respecting you all that much more, it's just that at times you make me feel as if you don't respect me and that in turn makes me feel uncomfortable and it's just that comfortability is at the forefront of any american's agenda and if you don't believe me then just ask rush limbaugh and those other self-satisfied, bumper-sticker mentality, capitalist-absorbed republicans

slipping it on

i'm going to try on my blackness one more time. ever since i've gotten these degrees and began using the term *vacation* as verb, I hadn't much use for it. it's almost like everyday a piece of me dies and i'm not talking about *keeping it real*, because if you, like i enjoy good comedy then we both ought to learn a thing or two about *keeping it real* from dave chappelle, but it's more like i'm not necessarily happy with the person i use to be, and i'm not quite satisfied with the person i've become, and still i'm longing and wanting to be that person i envision holding intellectual conversation, that person i envision whose books don't necessarily fly off the shelf but somehow affect and create positive change in others, and although i don't know the reasoning behind it, i've seem to have outgrown my blackness or its shrunk in size because as of late, i've begun to notice even the slightest things, like i started to view ms. condoleezza rice as more of a friend and less of a republican, and perhaps one of the craziest things is that president bush doesn't seem to annoy me as much and war has even begun to make more of a sensible solution when approaching global problems because "those people" don't get it and probably never will. but i stop, sadly thinking it wasn't too long ago that i, too, was categorized as "those people" and they never thought i'd get it, but i did and as i'm sitting here with all these degrees and accolades, i'm even wondering what exactly was it that i had gotten and why exactly are we fighting and then i remember parts of my christian childhood where muslims were always categorized as "those people" and i didn't quite understand why they were "those people" and we were those other people, and if we were they as if we had been apportioned to lead and they who were actually identified as those had resisted to follow and now pray to a different invisible man than i or we did, so we ought to love them until they reject our beliefs and then we are to hate them and then bomb them and then rape and then kill most of the men off and then send missionaries over there first and spread the gospel and force feed them pork and jesus and euro-catholicism or the newer more secular version, christianity.

in an attempt

in an attempt
to keep her happy
i would
keep a house
where i would sweep floors
and wash dishes daily

in an attempt
to keep her happy
i would
tiptoe
into her dreams
where i would embody the man
she had always
wanted me to be

but of late
i've learned
that her happiness
does not begin
with the washing
of a single dish
or the sweeping
of a single tile

one still moment

i think of you here, but soon you will be gone
i may shed a tear, but i, too, must keep on
the presence of you being here will surely be missed
just the vague thought of you brings a sudden bliss

these feelings i have for you
are filled with compassion because i care
in the eye of reality you may be gone,
but in my heart you are still here

may our friendship diminish never
but that we shall be friends forever
i care for you very deeply, but it is oh so silent
you will be gone soon,
but if only time were one still moment

snow days

as a child
i can *re   member*
friendships being crystallized
while skating to school
on sheets of ice
holding onto hands of peers
blanketed by grandma-knitted mittens
and bushes for dear life
only to find out
upon our unanticipated arrival at school
that our teacher was unable to attend
due to the weather conditions

effects
(for the cause)

late night phone conversations
fatigued mornings
lowered quiz scores
missed classes
genuine happiness
wandering daydreams
cell phone overage charges
intimacy
selfless text messages

she ignorantly roams around my world
guiltlessly unaware that she is the cause

pastime

i told her i was afraid of commitment
i told her i was fearful of falling in love
and of no one being there to catch me
she then turned and grabbed me
placed me in the comfort of her assurance
in the comfort of her arms
and told me i was safe

and without the use
of bats, balls, gloves, bases, diamond-shape fields,
or things as american as popcorn, cracker-jacks, and hot dogs
she suddenly became my favorite

pastime

rain

rain is god's sperm
dripping from the sky
into the receptive womb
of mother nature

she nurtures our very existence

yes?
(that is, if god is a man)

involuntarily

i want to be
the involuntary happiness
that interrupts
your bleak moments of sadness

a love supreme
(for she who is constantly exhausting the possibilities)

love is knowing it's u
without even having to look
through the peephole whenever i hear a knock

love is the scent of u that resides in the fabric
of my clothing while hanging in my closet

love is i making u
a warm bowl of campbell's soup
with saltine crackers on the side
it's the softness of my hand
rubbing vicks vapor rub
on the center of your chest
in an attempt to nurse u back to health
it's i tucking u in
and kissing u goodnight on your forehead
no matter how many birthdays pass

love is the conversations we hold
not necessarily for the words spoken
but for those that are not needed

love is the sun beaming down on us
and u catching me smiling over at u
for no particular reason

love is u answering your phone
but never talking too long
while i silently nibble

on the lower part of your neck
and quietly arrange kisses
on the crest of your collarbone
while softly rubbing the small of your back
and u do smile and make gentle faces
and softly caress my ear lobe
besides u and i both know
there probably wasn't a need to
because the hints held in your voice
told him that i was there anyway

love is sweating out your braids, your perm,
your twist, your mid-semester frustrations
on a cold wintry evening

love is what we make
in the middle of a spring afternoon
with the window blinds up
or in the still hours of the night
when i penetrate u
and u so happily receive me
and u and i become we
and we become one like the trinity

love is feeling and not quite being able to fully explain

love is engaging in verbal intimacy
u and i both sharing past secrets and future fears
of uncertainty at 3 o'clock in the morning

love is the way u fit so perfectly
in the crook of my arm when we sleep
it's only u knowing that i jump in my sleep
and laugh when i'm nervous

love is awaking to u staring at me
while resting in the ease of morning
watching the sun creep over, into,
and through the window sill
planting kisses on our cheeks whispering to awake

love is knowing that u flare your nose
when angry, cry when frustrated,
and curse when at a loss for words
shut me out when fed up
and allow me to come back in
when u don't necessarily want to but need to

in some cases, right or wrong,
love is even understanding that
loving you is not not loving her
it's more along the lines of
i love to not have to not
be away from you for moments at a time
and some may think this stanza
is about unfaithfulness and deceit
or about word play
but this has very little to do with charming words
and trickery of either language or action
and very much to do with divine purpose
and ms. faubert, who just so happened
to be my 3rd grade math teacher
at the full gospel christian school
taught me that the square root of 9
plus the square root of 16 = 7
and that 7 is a sign of divinity
then despite the "he said, she said"
we actually could be onto something

and i thought i ought
to share that with you in case
you ever wonder why
i never wonder why
and come so quickly whenever you call
or say you need me

love is stargazing in the coolness of a summer breeze
while resting on blankets of emotional security

love is u because u see through the fictitious laughs
and recognize the temporality of my ever-fading grin
that dissolves as quickly as cotton candy on a rainy day

i grow tired of masquerading

loving u is realizing that i am
simply because u are
but also acknowledging
that i am all that i am
and all that i am yet to become
because u are the embodiment
of endless possibilities   u enable me

love is u excavating the cave of my insecurities,
exhausting the possibilities with the hope of finding one we fit

loving u is completeness

it's me in need of a something emotionally tangible
one that can sustain this flawed existence
as we embark on this tragic journey we call romance

i want to love u perfectly in all your imperfection

quite simply put: love is u   *[period]*

BRANDON M. GRAHAM is an educator, writer, and hailed as an important voice in a group of "young, promising intellectuals," dedicated to improving the political, social, and academic landscape. Graham is a scholar, longtime lecturer, and an author who unswervingly addresses issues of race, culture, and relationships.

Several journals and newspapers have written articles on him and his work including *The New York Times, USA Today, The Hartford Courant, The Connecticut Post,* and *The New Haven Register.* He has taught seminars and conducted workshops on poetry, creativity, and the importance of literature, and belongs to several progressive African-American groups including *Matah Networks, NAACP, National Association of Black Journalists, INROADS, National Urban League,* and various subcommittees concerned with issues affecting black Americans.

He was born in Freeport, Illinois, and raised in Chicago, Dallas, various parts of Connecticut, and now resides in New York City. Graham holds a Bachelor of Science degree in English with a concentration in Writing, and an MBA with a concentration in Strategic Management both from Sacred Heart University.

From his days of performing throughout various parts of the country, he has secured for himself a national reputation. According to various scholars across the country, Graham offers the lyrical equivalent to that of the world-renowned "princess of black poetry", Nikki Giovanni, speaking to the heart of the human condition while carrying the rhythmic language of contemporary powerhouse Saul Williams.